the
Nanny Connie Way

the
Nanny Connie Way

Secrets to Mastering
the First Four Months of Parenthood

CONNIE SIMPSON

GALLERY BOOKS
New York London Toronto Sydney New Delhi

This publication contains the opinions and ideas of its author. It is intended to provide helpful and informative material on the subjects addressed in the publication. It is sold with the understanding that the author and publisher are not engaged in rendering medical, health, or any other kind of personal professional services in the book. The reader should consult his or her medical, health, or other competent professional before adopting any of the suggestions in this book or drawing inferences from it.

The author and publisher specifically disclaim all responsibility for any liability, loss, or risk, personal or otherwise, which is incurred as a consequence, directly or indirectly, of the use and application of any of the contents of this book.

G

Gallery Books
An Imprint of Simon & Schuster, Inc.
1230 Avenue of the Americas
New York, NY 10020

First Gallery Books trade paperback edition April 2018

GALLERY BOOKS and colophon are registered trademarks of Simon & Schuster, Inc.

For information about special discounts for bulk purchases, please contact Simon & Schuster Special Sales at 1-866-506-1949 or business@simonandschuster.com.

The Simon & Schuster Speakers Bureau can bring authors to your live event. For more information or to book an event, contact the Simon & Schuster Speakers Bureau at 1-866-248-3049 or visit our website at www.simonspeakers.com.

Interior design by Davina Mock-Maniscalco

Manufactured in the United States of America

10   9   8   7   6   5   4   3   2   1

Library of Congress Cataloging-in-Publication Data
Names: Simpson, Connie, author.
Title: The Nanny Connie Way / Connie Simpson.
Description: New York : Gallery Books, [2018]
Identifiers: LCCN 2017058400 (print) | LCCN 2017060075 (ebook) | ISBN 9781501184932 (ebook) | ISBN 9781501184925 (trade pbk. : alk. paper)
Subjects: LCSH: Infants—Care. | Parent and infant. | Child rearing. | Parenting.
Classification: LCC HQ774 (ebook) | LCC HQ774 .S547 2018 (print) | DDC 649/.1—dc23
LC record available at https://lccn.loc.gov/2017058400

ISBN 978-1-5011-8492-5
ISBN 978-1-5011-8493-2 (ebook)

To the many shoulders upon which I stand: great-great-grandma Hannah; great-grandma Lucy; grandma Catherine; grandpa Tom and grandma Gladys; my mom, Aliece; my dad, David; my angel, Mu; and, leaving no unturned stones, my aunts. Last but not least, my greatest achievement, my Henny Pen.

contents

Download The Nanny Connie Way AR App!

In 3 easy steps, you can download The Nanny Connie Way AR App and bring Connie right into your very own home!

Every chapter begins with an icon that when triggered, allows you to watch videos of Nanny Connie as if she were your own personal nanny, imparting her wisdom and love in her easy instructional tutorials on how to Just Be the Parent.

Step 1: Go to your app store and download The Nanny Connie Way AR app—it's free!

Step 2: Create a log-in and grant the app access to your camera.

Step 3: Just point your camera at each chapter icon, and Nanny Connie will appear!

(Try it out on the cover to meet Nanny Connie!)

introduction

I know nothing about my celebrities before taking care of their babies—that is, of course, except for my sweet baby Brooke Shields. Hell, who didn't want a pair of those Calvin Klein jeans?

I don't keep up with the movies or the music my A-listers put out. If I'm not listening to one of my lullaby compilations, I'm jamming to Aretha Franklin, Earth, Wind and Fire, Donny Hathaway, Nancy Wilson, Curtis Mayfield, or Prince. So, when I enter my celebrity homes for the first time, I tell them nine times out of ten I can damn sure guarantee I haven't seen or heard their work. And all of them, from Matt Damon to Justin Timberlake, give me the same gut laugh in response to my honesty.

I've cared for more than 270 families and worked in the homes of celebrities, CEOs of Fortune 500 companies, Young Presidents' Organization members, congressmen, foreign dignitaries, the owner of Ruby Tuesdays, the former CEO of the Chicago Mercantile Exchange, the Collier Family who saw the beauty of the Everglades and developed Collier County, and even the granddaughter of the inventor of the lava lamp. But a parent—even one who is still rocking her Calvins after two sweet babies—is a parent is a parent. And all parents need help! No matter their status, all my families only wanted to be the best parents to their children, and that was the glue that bonded us together for life.

I've been asked many times what it is like to work with so many people in the public eye. The answer is simple: It doesn't matter who my families are—they all need the same advice. Nothing more and nothing less. The Nanny Connie Way is for all parents.

This really hit home when I went to Dallas to work with one of my sweet moms, Catherine Rose. She was very quiet and soft-spoken, tending to the needs of everyone in her family as well as her outside obligations as a local philanthropist.

I normally sit with my moms when it's time to feed the baby, just to chew the fat and keep them from thinking about the baby tugging on their breast. One day as Catherine and I were talking, I glanced over to the stack of magazines on the coffee table. "God bless them," I'd say to myself as I finished each one, knowing I could not wear any of the tiny clothes or expensive shoes or even imagine carrying the money that went inside the purses, much less the purse itself.

"Hmm," I said, "I think one of my favorite magazines is missing." And this, my children, is where Nanny Connie proceeded to insert her foot into her mouth and told Catherine I called it The Book of Needless Markups.

She simply smiled and continued to see if I could put my other foot in my mouth as well. I was like, "I don't understand why it's so overpriced. It's unbelievable that someone would buy anything at that price, not to mention the crazy ideas they have for their Christmas catalogue." Listen, I was giving her the Nanny Connie rundown. As you young folks like to say, I was hatin'! Now the whole time I'm running my riot act, Catherine Rose was just smiling and laughing at me.

When I was done, in her very soft-spoken way, she said, "My grandfather was Marcus of Neiman Marcus." She dropped the mic on me! Yes, the magazine I had the love/hate relationship with was the Neiman Marcus catalogue, and yes, I was reading the riot act of my love/hate relationship to the granddaughter of Mr. Marcus himself. Let me tell you, if I could have dug a hole from Dallas to Mobile, I would've!

Catherine was one of those moms who taught me I shouldn't judge a book by its cover. She put me in my place and helped me understand that all parents are just that, PARENTS, and the outside world does not matter.

For more than three decades, I have been teaching parents just like you the basics for their newborns. I have been in the trenches with them all, from parents who barely had a roof over their heads to parents gracing the covers of magazines. My focus while working with all of these families is not only about making sure their babies thrive, but also that the parents succeed as well.

Nothing will compare to the sheer bliss and overwhelming love you'll feel when you gaze upon the face of your precious newborn and marvel at the tiny little fingers and toes. Can this amazing baby really be yours?

And nothing will compare to the sheer, overwhelming panic that will set in as soon as that gorgeous little baby starts crying inconsolably in what feels like surround sound, followed by the jumbled thoughts of *OMG! I am the parent now, and there is nobody here to help me!*

Don't hit the panic button! You're supposed to be scared! Taking care of a newborn is a brand-new job that has you sailing off into uncharted waters. That's why I've written this book for you. It's why I am here to snatch you up, give you a great big metaphorical hug, and reassure you that you will be fine—and your baby will be, too!

IT TAKES A VILLAGE

I am a proud product of the Deep South. There, I was taught the importance of manners and learned the values of knowledge, wisdom, compassion, love, and patience in abundance. Nurturing is something that was instilled in me through my family and Southern heritage. I was taught this just as I was taught to prepare dinner or say my prayers or do my daily chores. These values have made me the baby nurse I am today.

I grew up surrounded by the love of a large extended family who instilled a strong work ethic in me and taught me it takes a village to raise a child. Nurturing is in my DNA—from my mother, Aliece Simpson, and my father, David Simpson's, great-grandmother, Grandma Hannah.

Grandma Hannah was a larger-than-life figure, dressed in her white knee-high stockings and hand-sewn dresses, her hair neatly tucked under a white turban. Her story, passed down through the generations, is that prior to coming to America, she was a house slave on the plantations in Africa, where she bore an unknown number of children. As were the standards in those times, slaves were viewed as nothing more than property to be separated with no regard to their families. Although presumably still in her twenties, she was considered past childbearing age and was sent to America. She would eventually come to know freedom in the United States and bear twelve more children. For the first time in her life, she did not have to dream of who her children would grow up to be. Living as a sharecropper, Grandma Hannah became a highly accomplished and nurturing midwife in her community of Deer Park, Alabama. Although I would never have the chance to meet her, as a young child taking trips with my grandmother to visit our family who still lived on Grandma Hannah's homestead, I would quietly play on the porch and listen to the stories they told, not knowing that our paths would one day be so intertwined.

My mother was graceful, compassionate, patient, and, most of all, a woman of God. She exuded the pure essence of love and saw no wrong in any human. All of those qualities translated into her role as a nurse. She was one of the first African American aides to be waivered in as a practical nurse in Mobile, Alabama. She tutored under the watchful eyes of the Sisters of Mercy at Mobile's African American hospital, St. Martin de Porres, and then worked as an LPN under one of the few African American physicians making house calls, before eventually moving to private-duty nursing. I would go along with her on some of those follow-up house calls and sit in the living room, waiting for her to finish up with her patients. She would bring out the best in everyone she came into contact with. You see, she had the most loving parents in Gladys and Tom Smith, even with them caring for all their eight kids. Without hesitation, my grandparents would give to others, be it children or families in the neighborhood. Their door was always open to someone in need.

As for me, after attending Mississippi University for Women, Mobile College, and Southern University in Baton Rouge, where I majored in early childhood education, I interrupted my studies to take care of my young daughter, Courtney, and then returned to school for further training in the Montessori Method. My career took many turns: I worked as a public-school substitute teacher, a grocery store baker, a public-school cafeteria employee, a summer lunch program organizer, and a small gumbo shop owner.

Eventually, I stepped out on the limb of faith with a woman I loved and respected, my cousin Ileaner Gipson Randall, affectionately known as Mu. She was more than just my cousin—she was everyone's mother. Like my mom, Mu was a woman of God who conveyed the pure essence of love, a nurturer who could take you at your worst and restore your soul. She instilled the importance of family pride, respect, and generosity not only in her children and grandchildren, but also in any and all she came into contact with. She gave me the confidence to shift gears.

After teaching at a local preschool, I began working as a baby nurse for two professional parents from a prominent family in Mobile who desperately needed help raising their newborn. I soon found myself in great demand as a local baby nurse.

Mu had reminded me that before certifications and degrees were available to African American women during slavery, and even as late as the 1960s, the word *nurse* meant "nurse back to health," not the clinical term we use today. I grew up surrounded by nurses and their loving wisdom, and I am honored to use that word to describe what I do.

My world of baby nursing took me from Huntsville, Alabama, to Dallas, Texas, to Washington, DC, to Hollywood, and no matter where I traveled, all parents had the same issues and faced the same hurdles—from setting a daily routine and trying to get their little ones to eat on a decent schedule to juggling their own personal and professional obligations while never seeming to get enough sleep.

I always tell my families I will give them all of the knowledge I have so we can get through the next three to six months together, because they can handle it. My families eventually learn that this larger-than-life woman living in their homes doesn't want anything more than to build a firm foundation for them and their new baby.

It's absolutely essential to pour a foundation that will become as sturdy and durable as your love for your baby. It's what you will build upon for the next eighteen years . . . and it's the first step to making your baby happy and healthy—and becoming an even happier and more resilient parent who can face whatever life throws your way.

Because every baby is unique and you're going to be learning on the job, I want you to know that everything is going be okay. Believe me, your baby is a lot stronger and smarter than you are. You can and will learn what to do.

HOW TO USE THIS BOOK

This book is divided into four parts to make it as easy as possible to find the information you need.

Part One gives you the essential, reassuring information you should know before the baby arrives. I'll tell you what items you do (and don't) need for baby care, who to hire and what to ask, how to arrange your schedule, and what to check off your pre-birth checklist so you'll be as prepared as possible once the baby arrives.

In Part Two, I'll tell you what to expect in the delivery room and in the immediate after-glow of your baby's birth.

Part Three is the operations manual for baby care, covering everything from latching on to diaper rash to my tried-and-true sleepy-time ritual that will have your baby conking out on a predictable schedule.

Part Four is the operations manual for parents. Taking the best possible care of you is just as important as feeding and nurturing your baby.

Jessica Biel: "Nanny Connie was with us every step of the insanely challenging way for the first year of our son's life. She sat up with me night after night while I struggled to breast-feed. She held my hand and my head as I sobbed and ached through postpartum. She told it like it was and somehow made me laugh when I thought there was absolutely nothing funny about any of this."

I wish I could take care of you and your baby the way I took care of all my families, but instead, I'm going to be there for you in every page of this book. Even if your partner is pretending to be asleep while the baby is screaming in the middle of the night, I'll be there. I'll be there when you and your baby are covered in pee, poop, and puke. I'll be there when you realize you put the car keys in the freezer because you're so exhausted from sleep deprivation. Yep, that will definitely happen. I'll be there with you when the side eyes cut across the restaurant because you dared to go out to eat with your child. I'll be there when passengers on a plane hold their breath, hoping you and Baby won't sit by them. And I'll definitely be there when you're sweating your tail off because you're fully covered and trying to breast-feed in public.

I'm ready because I know you can do this!

This book is going to give you not just the advice you crave, but also the reassurance that will empower you to become the best, the strongest, and the most phenomenal parent to your little one. It's not just about making you the parent you want to be—it's about making you the parent you have to be. Before you know it, you're going to be rocking your baby's world with confidence and love.

While you can't have me (or my hugs!) helping you feed and take care of your precious newborn, you can have the very best of my years of experience and knowledge in these pages. This book is what I've learned from being in the lab for thirty years. My oldest "baby" is now thirty-seven years old, and I still get phone calls from her, so I can talk her off her own parenting meltdown ledge.

Let's get to nurturing!

part one

BUN IN THE OVEN

Everything You Need to Do Before the Baby Is Born

BUT BEFORE YOU START: MY TOP-TEN LIST SO YOU CAN BE PPP (PREPARED, PATIENT, AND PHENOMENAL)

Jessica Biel: "The phrase I remember that most accurately categorizes my experience with Nanny Connie is 'Hell nah, dawg.' She would say that to me over and over. She'd say that to me when I'd bring her a book with some generic piece of advice or when I would come to her with some goofy home remedy a friend of a friend would recommend. 'Hell nah, dawg,' she would say, roll her big loving eyes, give me an all-knowing grin, and send me on my way."

1 Trust your instincts. Don't second-guess yourself, because your instincts will be right 99.9 percent of the time. You should try not to listen to everyone who's eager to give you advice. I know this is hard. Don't get me wrong: some information is good, but most people won't know which of their opinions will be helpful to you or not.

2 Stress makes everything 200 percent worse. Take a few deep breaths, don't rock the boat, put both oars in the water, be calm, and you will make it to the shore. This is nothing but another test, and the sooner you realize there are a lot of aspects of baby care that are out of your control, the sooner you can find ways to minimize the stress.

3 Did you know that the word *parent* is plural? Well, it is! I'm going to teach all parents how to get the self-confidence they deserve and to be on the same page at the same time to avoid creating what you want to avoid (see number 2!).

4 Newborns are smart! That umbilical cord has an amazing amount of power that you likely don't even realize exists, and this means babies know much more than you think they know. Don't be short-changed by your newborn; that lifeline called the umbilical cord has connected them in more ways than you can imagine. Those crazy somersaults and karate kicks that you felt weren't just for fun. When you think about it, those nights you stayed up late, poured on that sriracha sauce, ate those chili peppers, or had your Waffle House hash browns smothered, covered, and chunked at 2:00 a.m. . . . I guess by now you get the point—it was the baby's way of conveying to you that they didn't agree with any of those decisions you were making. Babies can hear very early in utero, too; it's as if *Horton Hears a Who* comes to life. They hear sounds when you're upset, when you're happy, even when you're playing your favorite music. If you play something soothing that makes you relax and feel good, your baby will pick right up on it and be relaxed and feel good, too.

5 Be patient. Raising a child is all about repetition. Remember learning your multiplication tables by reciting them over until you were saying them in your sleep? Well, you're in the classroom of life now, and what you're doing . . . and doing . . . and doing is going to stick.

6 Your new favorite word is *practical*. You don't need to live in Baby Merchandise World. What's inside the package is not going to rule the world. Your child is going to rule the world. So, all this stuff (especially clothes) won't matter because your baby is going to outgrow it in a week. (Whoever invented dry-clean-only clothing for newborns clearly never had one!)

7 Babies need regular round-the-clock feedings. Babies need changing. Babies need comfort. All of these things are going to wake up your baby. Until a child is old enough to run his own bathwater, know that there will be sleepless nights. There will be teething pains, overloaded diapers, night terrors, and just the fact that some nights, babies need a little extra love from their parents.

BABY CARE WITH JESSICA ALBA AND CASH WARREN

Some of my best moments are with my last-minute parents who aren't quite sure if they want a baby nurse or a night nurse. They normally have read all the books and attended all the classes, yet once they come home with that bundle of joy, reality hits them like a brick. This shoe fits one of my adorable families, Jessica Alba and Cash Warren. Little Miss Honor had made her official arrival, and I received the Nanny Call (like Batman, just a tad bit less dramatic). During Honor's first night home, she was on her best behavior. Cash and Jessica figured night two would be the same. They had the cradle next to the bed, and I was just down the hall. During the night, I heard Honor cry and made it about halfway down the hall when I heard feet shuffling in their room. The door never opened, so I turned around and said to myself, "Leave them alone; they're fine." The farther I walked down the hall toward my room, the louder the sweet little cries became. I kicked myself for not reaching out because I knew exactly what was going on. Honor had gas and needed to be repositioned and swaddled. She just wanted a little help figuring out her comfort zone. I went to the door, knocked very gently, peeked in, and offered some advice. We got Honor settled, and I headed back to my neck of the woods.

About four or five minutes later, sweet little Honor was making her presence known, a bit louder and prouder this time. I listened for a while and headed back into the room. Jessica was trying her best to save the situation, and I knew exactly how she was feeling. Cash had this look of a mix between the fear of God and a deer in headlights on his face. I offered some advice, but before leaving the room, I said, "If you guys will let me have her, I can figure out what is going on, and you both can get some rest." Cash looked at Jessica, and Jessica looked at Cash. And that's when I found out Cash must have been a track and field star. He jumped clean across his wife's side of the bed and cleared the walkway in the process. Before I could make it to the door, he had the cradle in his hand and was waiting on me to walk down the hall!

8 Your baby is only this little once. The early months won't come again, and even though you may be exhausted now,

believe me when I say you will miss it someday. Is it important for your baby to hit those milestones? Of course. But to be early with those milestones? That's hit or miss. Enjoy your child and savor the moment. Even the middle-of-the-night-will-I-ever-sleep-again moments.

9 I've never been a great chess player. In fact, I've never been a chess player, but since working with my babies, I have learned to play chess—which actually just means you need to be prepared. You need to learn to stay three moves ahead of your children because they always think three moves ahead. This is the test of being a phenomenal parent. You'll know you're on top of it. You'll know you can conquer the world.

10 Most important, that new human being who has been brought into this world chose you. They wanted to give you all the love, care, and attention they received in the heavens above. Embrace your newborn, and they will embrace you. Your baby loves and trusts you. Always!

And here is one to grow on:

Over my many years of working with some of the most wonderful babies and families in the world, one of the most important things I've taught them is Life Happens and for those who know the other saying, Shit Happens, too. Know your stuff, because knowledge is power. The only way you can prepare for the unexpected is to know it will happen. There are going to be numerous times you're going to be pushed out of your comfort zone, and you're just going to have to realize that you need to go with the flow.

Your baby is not an alien from another planet—this newborn has inherited the genetic makeup of both parents. After working with so many families, I've realized that this is majorly overlooked. Some newborns come into the world and sleep like a dream; others come into the world and have every reason to be uncomfortable. One newborn may have inherited the acid reflux of one parent and the three-hour sleep schedule of the other parent, not to mention an allergy to everything on the face of the earth, taking after their aunt.

This all takes time to figure out, so put on your best wading boots, make that pot of coffee, and stop blaming yourself and listening to the peanut gallery. In other words, babies have a really great way of putting your ass in check. No matter how much money you have, no matter how many books you've read, no matter how much you think you know about babies, your sweet little one will bring you right back to reality. They don't care if you're sleep-deprived, sore, or cranky. They have no filters, and they don't know when they're supposed to be good. They're still that cake baking in the oven—but if you cry and cry because you wanted that perfect Martha Stewart cake, but you got that half-baked Betty Crocker version, you'll be setting yourself up for failure. And the only person you'll be hurting is you.

The truth is the truth. It is never going to change, and babies are never going to change. So, if Plan A isn't working and the cake didn't rise (or, in your case, the baby came early, and you didn't have the birth you wanted, or your mother-in-law is being just a tad too critical), well, honey, you just move along to Plan B, and that cake will rise. You'll be happy. The baby will be happy. Life will be sweet as cake.

Remember, the very best parent to your baby is you.

chapter one

ASSEMBLY REQUIRED

Getting Your Home Ready for Baby

> *I would always* give Lucy Damon the rundown on keeping her girls safe: putting undershirts on them, cushions on the sharp corners of the tables, and Plexiglas on the stairs. Every time I would come to Lucy with a new safety concern, she would laugh and say, "All right Non, between you and Matt, we are going to bubble wrap the kids."

Getting ready for Baby is one of the most important things you can do to make the adjustment to your little one that much easier. I can't stress this enough. Try as best you can to follow the instructions in this chapter, and you will be so thankful (and feel so accomplished) when you have crossed these tasks off your to-do list.

SETTING UP THE BABY'S AREAS

How much stuff do you really need for the baby? Some items are essential, but there is no need to go overboard with every new piece of equipment you see online or hear about from other parents. This is what's really important:

+ **Ease of use.** This means practicality. You are going to be on call for the baby 24/7, so anything that requires fidgeting with buttons or is hard to use at three o'clock in the morning when the baby has just woken up for the third time that night will end up with you screaming in frustration before throwing it in the trash.

+ **Comfort.** Buy items and furniture that are comfortable—not just for Baby, but for you!

+ **Preparedness.** When an explosion has just filled a diaper and the sweet aroma (ha!) hits your nostrils, the last thing you want is to be stooped over a changing table that gives you a backache because it's the wrong height—and then you realize you've run out of wipes!

+ **Organization.** Keep your essentials in the same place and arranged in the order you use them. Take this pre-baby time to clear out any clutter. Nothing beats coming home with your new little one to a clean, tidy, and organized house. It will free you up to take care of your baby without worrying where you put the burp cloths. Enjoy this time, because once your baby is a toddler, "clean and tidy" will be distant memories!

BONUS TIP

Overflow. Make sure you have an area (a closet, drawer, cabinet) where you keep your "overflow" items. Think of it as a stockroom with a detailed inventory. Everyone who checks it should know what needs to be replaced. This will help everyone from your partner to your babysitter keep supplies stocked.

Feeding Stations

Your feeding station is as important as how and when you feed the baby. This should be a room or area that is not in a high-traffic spot in your home and is a very comfortable sitting area for you. You should be able to spread out your newborn if you need to change a diaper or let her lie down safely to wake up to feed. If you have the space, the other side of your bedroom is a great place.

The last thing you want is to settle in to feed and all the house traffic starts to walk through the room. In the very beginning, breast-feeding is like starting a new relationship. It has to be caressed and formed without any outside distractions. You don't want the whole world having a front-row seat to something that intimate. This is not *The Bachelor*! Get your act together first. There will be plenty of time to show the world your new-found love!

Every feeding station should be stocked like you're settling in to watch your favorite movie. You should have snacks and lots of water. As a breast-feeding mother, you need lots of water. Hydrate, hydrate, hydrate! Remember: breast milk is 75 percent water. Now, I don't know who you think is going to put that water in your breast milk if you're not drinking it. Get ready to guzzle!

The feeding station essentials include:

+ Water

+ Gas drops

+ Burp cloths

+ Nipple cream

+ Breast pads

+ Hand sanitizer

+ Swaddle blankets

+ Feeding pillow

+ Phone for SOS calls only

+ Diapers

+ Changing pad

+ Wipes

+ Butt paste

Remind yourself that the water for you and the diapers for the baby are must-haves. With a newborn, diaper explosions during feedings are probable. I can't tell you the number of times I've had moms start feeding, and in less than two minutes, their newborn's face draws up, they stop eating, and, all of a sudden, an explosion like no other proceeds from the other end. If I had a dollar for all the expressions the parents had on their faces when they get that first explosive cottage-cheese diaper! Don't be surprised if you need to change two to three diapers during a feeding. (For more on pee and poop, see p.134 in chapter 7.)

Changing Stations

There is no such thing as too many changing stations! You can put them wherever you like, and I recommend that if you have a two-story house, you have one on each floor. Your baby's changing stations don't necessarily need to be in the baby's room. Put them in the area of your home where you'll be spending the most time with the baby. (Parents who live in small apartments often don't get separate changing tables because they don't have room, but a sturdy table with a changing mat on top works just as well.)

Make sure your changing station has some type of nonskid protection underneath the changing cushion. Surfaces like wood are very slippery, and the last thing you want is your baby flying one way and the diaper adding a new accent color to your wall.

Stocking the Changing Table

A fully stocked changing table is important to your survival. Have these essentials on hand at all times. Remember to replenish the stocks at the end of each day so you don't have to worry about running out of anything in the middle of the night.

+ 12 diapers

+ Plain water wipes

+ Butt cream

+ Extra change of clothes

+ Socks

+ Burp cloths

+ Swaddles

+ Gas drops

+ Lotion (shea butter)

+ Any additional meds (Motrin, Tylenol, etc.)

+ Nasal aspirator

+ Laundry basket

+ Thermometers (rectal and ear/forehead)

+ Hand sanitizer

Diaper Disposal

A diaper pail is just that—a diaper pail! You don't need anything expensive and high-tech, because the more complicated it is, the more you'll find yourself being the only one dealing with it—and I'll bet my last dollar you and your partner have touted how you are going to do this together. Don't set yourself or your partner up for failure because the diaper pail looked really cute in the store or the peanut gallery recommended it. Practical is much more important at this point. Don't narrow yourself to having to find a specific disposal bag of the same brand, as the bags can get pricey. I highly recommend a diaper disposal like the Diaper Champ because it's easy access, and you can use your everyday plastic trash bags in it.

Play Areas

You can start playing with your baby right away! (See more in chapter 9.) A play area is very mobile and small at first and can be as simple as a basket or drawer. Keep some toys near your feeding area and where you tend to sit with your infant. You will be more likely to read and play if they're close by.

SETTING UP THE BABY'S ROOM

The Furniture You Need—and the Furniture You Don't

I can't tell you how many times I have walked into a baby's nursery and found something straight out of a magazine. It's absolutely gorgeous. I never want to burst a parent's bubble about their nursery, especially when I can see the love and care that went into setting it up. But is an antique wooden rocking chair with hard, sharp edges practical? Sure, it spoke to you in the store and went perfectly with the décor, but I'm here to tell you the only additions it's going to add in the long run are a number of banged chins, leg bruises, and dislocated toes. Eventually that rocker will become known as that damn chair! Remember, keep it functional. The biggest question you need to ask yourself is "Is it practical?"

Here is the one piece of furniture you really need: a very comfy daybed, love seat, or small sofa. This will be your second home when you come into the nursery for those nights when cozy cuddles are needed. As your little one gets older, it's the perfect space for reading. I know you're thinking a chair works, too, but it's not good for sleeping in—and there will be many nights when you'll be grateful you chose the couch.

Take your time choosing! Test different options for your comfort and be sure it's easily cleaned, as you know it's bound to get stained! The baby will sleep in a bassinet for about the first four months, so this is actually a great time for you to finish decorating your nursery. As your baby grows, you'll have a better idea of what you truly need. This will save you lots of money and time in the long run.

Bassinets and Co-Sleepers

A bassinet is essential. Your baby will sleep in it for their first three to four months. It can easily be moved from room to room, and it's travel-friendly, so the baby will conk right out no matter where it is, as it smells all milky and delicious and feels familiar. Some brands such as BabyBjörn come sudden infant death syndrome (SIDS)-approved, meaning they have mesh siding to improve breathability. I prefer this brand because it is lightweight, stable, accessible, breathable, and easily assembled. If BabyBjörn is out of your price range, the Graco Pack 'n Play with a bassinet and changing table is another great option.

Although they aren't easily portable, co-sleepers are also great. They attach to the side of your bed and give you easy access to your baby for breast-feeding—without the risk of rolling over on them. Some co-sleepers do have the SIDS-approved mesh siding. However, I strongly recommend a watchful eye for a bassinet or a co-sleeper regardless of the SIDS approval. My favorite is the Arm's Reach co-sleeper.

Moses Baskets

Moses baskets look adorable, and parents like them because their handles allow you to easily move the baby from one room to another. But I don't recommend them because they're too flimsy and soft on the sides and don't have the support of a bassinet. I've seen babies roll over into the little cracks or roll around even though parents thought it was on a level surface. I'm actually more fearful of a baby being in a Moses basket than lying on a bed.

Cribs

You don't need a crib until your baby is close to six months old—which is great news because you'll know what you'll like by that point. Crib must-haves are:

+ Easily adjustable parts
+ Slats that are close together

+ A good-fitting mattress

+ Ability to withstand the test of your child at the Terrible Two stage (yes, that's real!)

+ Forgiving wood for head-bangers

Crib Bedding

+ Get a standard firm mattress that fits tightly in the crib.

+ Babies leak! Put a waterproof pad atop the mattress. Buy at least two breathable ones. Naturepedic has a great selection of mattresses and waterproof pads.

+ Top that with your sheets. They should be organic and made from natural fibers only, if possible.

+ Never place pillows in the crib, ever.

+ Don't use bumpers, either. Babies can get wedged under them and suffocate. When they're older, they can choke on or get strangled by the ties. If you insist on bumpers, make sure they are mesh only.

+ Don't buy dust ruffles, mini comforters, or duvets! A cotton baby blanket with a loose weave is best. A lot of parents like sleep sacks, a new way of swaddling that offers the same benefits, so they don't have to worry about blankets.

Don't Rock My Baby

Trust me on this: Do not get a rocking chair!

I am a Southerner through and through and I love my rocking chairs—just not for you to rock your new baby in! The constant rocking, swaying, and bouncing can set you up for disaster. If you're trying to keep a baby awake to eat, the soothing motion of a rocker will do just the opposite.

Don't get me wrong—being comfortable is vital to breast-feeding or bottle feeding. But if you start all the rocking now, you'll constantly have to rock for all your feedings. You should not implement the rocking chair until you and your infant know each other—meaning you have control over how to soothe them in any situation. Don't let the rocking chair have the control. If you don't, you'll find yourself doing the rock walk to settle down every cry. Rocking is a much harder habit to break than it is to start. Start how you want to finish.

Clothing Organization

I love helping with clothing organization—it's deeply satisfying to put everything in its place.

An organized closet means you'll know where all the essentials are. And you'll get into the much-needed habit of restocking after you change the baby's diaper and clothes versus you wanting to chop off your partner's head because they can't find that one outfit that you've been waiting to put your baby in. Remember: it's chess, not checkers! I didn't get this gray hair by sitting on the corner collecting wooden nickels.

The changing-station drawers should be filled with onesies, nightwear, diapers, wipes, rubber pads, sleep sacks, and socks. This way, you'll have everything you need, especially at night, when you're dressing your baby.

How to Organize Your Baby's Closet

+ Organize the closet by the baby's age, from newborn to six months, and by season. Label the sections according to each month—these visuals really help.

+ Everything that can be put on a hanger should be put on one, so you see the items easily and don't miss anything. Babies grow so fast that they often will size out of many of the adorable little onesies you have before you've had a chance to put them on, so make sure items are hung separately.

+ Create sections for shirts, mated socks, pants, sweaters, shorts, dresses, etc.

+ When babies have outgrown their clothing, it's best to label your sentimental pieces and put them away in a memory storage box. Donate the remaining items to family or organizations that assist families in need.

BABY EQUIPMENT FOR THE HOUSE

Bouncy Seat

A bouncy seat can be very entertaining when used in moderation. In fact, if your baby likes it, it can actually be your extra pair of hands—but not your babysitter! (No toy should ever be your babysitter.) Get one with black and white images, toys across the front, and/or a place for a mobile. There is no need to buy batteries because you shouldn't be using that function anyway. (Think of the bouncy seat as a rocking chair!) You want your baby to be comfortable and content—not a martini (shaken, not stirred).

Swings

I don't do swings. See, that was easy! If you do want to try one, go ahead. Use one at a friend's house and consider it only if your baby likes it.

Boppy

These are great when your baby is not yet mobile, as it keeps them safe and secure if you want to place them in the middle of the bed or floor. Once babies start wiggling and giggling, though, Boppies start to serve a different purpose, and you will have to be a lot more attentive. (Boppies are also great for breast-feeding to help support the baby's weight. Some of my moms have found that they used the Boppy more for breast-feeding than anything else!)

Play Gym

A colorful blanket with some toys and an unbreakable plastic mirror can accomplish the same thing, but play gyms are worth the buy. They should be black and white and have facial features—our learning process starts as early as the newborn stage. I rank them up there with mobiles, which you can read about in chapter 9.

Exersaucers

I love exersaucers, but you can't use them until the baby has full head control, which is about the time they outgrow the bouncy seat (five to six months). If you have the space for it, go ahead and get one now. They are a good form of sensory overload, as they engage the baby's attention by working their legs, turning their bodies, moving their hands, and coordinating their eyes.

BABY EQUIPMENT FOR GOING OUTSIDE

This is one area where you need to do your homework, but it all comes down to personal preference—and, as ever, durability and practicality. Just remember that what's ideal for some parents might not be good for you due to a whole host of reasons (size, cost, design, etc.). Have fun shopping. It's all part of the antici-pation!

Don't, however, think this is going to be a one-stop shop or that you're successfully buying everything you need for the next two to three years. This will basically change every two to three weeks until you get it right. It can leave you scratching your head and other places, if you know what I mean, with frustration. (That's what you get for following the damn peanut gallery. Oops, I said that out loud again . . . !)

Infant Carriers and Car Seats

Two of the most important items you will need are an infant carrier and a car seat. The absolute most important aspect for both is their installation. It doesn't matter how highly rated or expensive a carrier or car seat is if it's not installed correctly. This puts your baby at grave risk should there be an accident.

Car seat installation is not an easy task. Avoid the hassle and the worries about correct attachment by going to a local police or fire station to ask for help. You can also go online to find a Safe Kids car seat checkup event in your community. Be sure that any-one who will have your child frequently has their own infant car-rier and/or car seat, and make sure their seat is properly installed in their vehicle, too. You never want to be in a position where your baby needs to go somewhere but can't because of the car seat.

Infant Carriers

You'll have plenty of choices. If you get one that snaps into the car seat as well as into a stroller, you will save yourself so much hassle and the extra expense. They must:

- ✦ Be rear facing.

- ✦ Tether.

- ✦ Have at least a four-star federal government rating, no matter the brand.

- ✦ Have a good recline, because most babies spend a lot of time in a car.

- ✦ Use the five-point lock system.

An infant carrier will last you at most four months. After that, you will be putting the baby right into the car seat. Why? Not only will the baby's weight put a lot of stress on your back and shoulders, but they'll also outgrow the carrier!

Car Seats

Graduating to a car seat is when you get all the bells and whistles. The brands I am familiar with are Britax, Nuna, and Graco, but you should spend as much time as you need researching all brands. These are the questions you need to consider:

- ✦ How far does it recline?

- ✦ Is it rear facing? (Children need to be rear facing until they are at least two years old, but you can put an unbreakable plastic mirror on it, so you can see the baby when you're driving.)

- ✦ Does it have a cup holder?

- ✦ Is the material breathable? A baby who's sweating it out in their seat is a baby who's going to get vocal about this discomfort!

- ✦ Does it use the five-point lock system?

✦ What is the maximum weight? (This will determine how long this seat will be in your life.)

✦ Is it easy to clean? (Trust me: this is a must!)

A LAND CRUISER NAMED CONNIE

You know that saying, "Don't mess with Texas"? Well my next mother, a straight-up Texan who loves her trucks, has this hanging in her house. Her Dodge with its club cab was her pride and joy. As soon as I saw it, I shook my head in a slow roll, gave her a shit-eater smile, and said, "Naw, dawg." (In this case, my thoughts were much more colorful than a "Naw, dawg," but I can't write that here!) I asked her where in her mind she thought we were going—because I didn't see us leaving the driveway. She assured me that the infant seat was going to ride just fine between those club cab seats. She even showed me her "extra room" by opening the club cab door. I shook my head and crossed my legs so I wouldn't pee myself from laughing.

The first time we took the baby to the pediatrician, we used her husband's car, but when we had to go to an airport salvage and only had her truck, the baby would have had to go in the back. I told her no way; it still wasn't safe. The car seat just couldn't be tethered properly in the cab, and she was going to have to get rid of that truck. I mumbled and cussed through the whole trip as she laughed at me, thinking she had won the battle. Truth be told, a part of my cussing was because I thought she was right! I was thinking nothing could change my thought process, but the airport salvage is a thrifter's gold mine and distracted me enough to get my mind off the club cab and the safety of my baby.

We had packed up and were headed back to the house

when her phone rang. Her husband was trying to figure out where we were and told us to pull over to the side of the road because he was on his way. We looked at each other and thought he was crazy! Five minutes later, he showed up. But we didn't recognize him because he was sitting inside of a shiny new black Land Cruiser. My cussing turned into words of joy. Now I started to laugh! Her husband took the truck, and she began cussing because she realized her truck was gone forever.

Now, however, all was well. We had a new baby and a safe car, and I had peace of mind. That's what I call a push gift!

Strollers

The perfect stroller is the Holy Grail in the parenting world. I wish I could tell you there is one model that'll have every single feature on your wish list, but you're out of luck! There are only trade-offs, so if you find a stroller that fulfills three of the five features on your list, then you are way ahead of the curve. For example, most running strollers don't fold, so if you don't have a lot of space to store more than one stroller, you'll need something smaller. If you have to make compromises now, you might not have to make them when your baby is bigger and your needs change.

How to Buy a Stroller

Make a list of features you want/need based on your activities, such as everyday use, travel, running, etc. For newborns, I like strollers where the baby can face the parent, which helps them to continue to know they still are connected to their parents in the crazy outside world. Think about the stuff you see on a daily basis as an adult that makes you say, "WTH." Don't impose those visuals on your newborn right off the bat. Remember, they're little sponges soaking in everything.

Buying a stroller is like buying a car; in two years (if that long), you are going to trade it in. By the time you're ready for your next stroller, the gotta-have-it features will have changed. Look for:

- ✦ Sturdy wheels.

- ✦ Brakes that are visible, so you use them! Even a very slight incline can cause a stroller to roll away, so train yourself to always put the brake on, even when the stroller is resting on a level surface.

- ✦ A nice big basket for storage under the seat.

- ✦ A decent recline so the baby can sleep.

- ✦ Versatility in facing your baby to either the front or back.

- ✦ Ease of use for you and your partner. If it's part of a snap-in infant carrier system, be sure it snaps in and out easily—it should feel and sound nice and loud (and safe!). It should also be easy to fold. I have plenty of stroller stories where the stroller broke, and Dad blamed the manufacturer, when it was actually his fault because he didn't know how to fold it properly and was too embarrassed to admit it!

- ✦ Adjustable height so everyone strolling your baby can do so comfortably.

On-Body Baby Carriers

Baby carriers aren't necessary if you have a good infant carrier, but they are convenient, especially if you're going someplace where an infant carrier or stroller isn't practical (city buses and subways, for example). There are many good ones (the BabyBjörn is my top pick), and the main thing to look for is comfort for you and your partner. Be sure to practice with it before the baby arrives so you know how to get it on and off quickly.

A lot of moms love hip slings as they take the weight off your shoulders, but they are dangerous to use if the baby's neck muscles aren't strong enough to hold up their head (this usually happens at five to six months), as tiny ones can suffocate if they are lying prone in a sling.

Once your little bundle arrives, you should practice placing them in the carrier over your bed or another soft area before you actually have to maneuver a baby in the carrier.

Diaper Bags

Here's how to choose a diaper bag: practicality! Forget the really pretty floral one or the one that's got lots of pockets but is kind of heavy. You want to think *Good Housekeeping*, not *Vogue*. This diaper bag is going to be your lifesaver when you go out with the baby, and it's gonna take a beating. Use this checklist:

✦ Practicality. Did I say that already? Yes, I did. This means it's lightweight yet durable.

✦ Ease of cleaning. Trust me: it's gonna get grimy. Your work-horse diaper bag is one that you can wipe down and turn inside out to clean out the milk that has turned into cottage cheese at the bottom or (yep) the stuff that oozed out of a leaky diaper. You're going to use it over and over, even when that vinyl starts cracking on the inside, so you want to have one that you can flip out, hang upside-down, and let dry.

+ Comfort. Does it feel good on your body?

+ Pockets, pockets, and pockets! Different-size pockets for different-size items work best. Some diaper bags have pockets on the outside just for wipes, which is a brilliant idea since you won't have to open the bag and go rooting around when the baby just had an explosion. Look for a small pocket for the pacifier you know you're going to forget. When your thoughts turn to mush, your fingers will still know where the essentials are.

+ Size. An enormous diaper bag that gives you lots of space means you'll dump the kitchen sink in there, too, but that extra poundage is gonna drag you down. You aren't just carrying a purse anymore—you've got a diaper bag, maybe a pump bag, and a baby to deal with!

+ Clear the clutter! Dump all the stuff that's accumulated in your purse and combine it with what's in your diaper bag, so you have one less thing to think about. What do you really need? Your wallet, keys, cell phone, a lipstick or lip balm, some tissues—that's it.

+ As with strollers, you will likely need more than one diaper bag as long as your baby is in diapers. Even the best ones get worn out.

+ If you have a hard time letting go of your purse, buy one super-practical diaper bag for daily use and a fancier one that looks like a purse for special occasions. It's like wearing nice comfy flats during the day and heels at night. But bear in mind that designer diaper bags are rarely as water-resistant as you'll want them to be.

+ Clear bags are essential. The last thing you want your diaper bag to be is a dumpster dive. Clear bags help you stay organized and will also help others more quickly find something in your bag.

Diaper Bag Essentials

+ Trash bags

+ Two different-colored pacifiers (In case you drop one, you won't get them mixed up.)

+ Baby sunscreen

+ Butt cream

+ Wipes

+ Baby's favorite toy or lovey

+ Rubber pad

+ Bibs

+ Baby sweater

+ Two burp cloths

+ Six diapers

+ Change of clothes

+ UV protector hat

+ Gas drops

+ Emergency contact list

+ Pump bag if you are breast-feeding or two bottles filled with formula and a small bottle of water

Don't forget to reload your diaper bag after every outing.

Pump Bags

A pump bag is not a diaper bag. It's much smaller and should only be used for your pump and milk storage—nothing else. You don't want it to get cluttered and prevent you from finding the most important parts of your pump when the baby is hungry and crying. Look for:

+ Easy access.

+ Some kind of cool spot that keeps the milk chilled. This is more essential than the pump because if you absolutely have to, you can hand-express milk, but you can't store it.

+ Something lightweight that you can wipe off. Don't go too fancy; all you need is a place for your pump and your milk.

+ Something memorable. You need to check and recheck the bag whenever you use it. I can't tell you how many moms have been meticulous in taking their pump bags to work but then come home and forget they have milk in it. The next day, not only does it stink, but the moms are devastated because they've pumped all this liquid gold and now it's trash because it sat in a bag all day. Don't cry when this happens to you—it happens to every mom I've ever worked with!

BABY PRODUCTS FOR DAILY USE

Diapers

When choosing a diaper, cheap is not always the best, and expensive is not always necessary. Organic diapers have come a long way, but I recommend Pamper Swaddlers and Honest Diapers, as they allow your newborn's bottom to breathe, preventing diaper rash.

✦ Newborns rarely stay in the newborn size for more than two or three weeks, if that. Once you jump into the next size, it should last for at least three to six weeks.

✦ Use a size larger than the age range your baby falls into in order to give them room. This will help prevent diaper rash, provide air circulation, and keep the poop a little bit farther away from your baby's sweet little tushie.

✦ Online bulk buying and delivery is a major modern-day miracle for stressed and overtired parents who don't have the energy to drag heavy bags of diapers home.

A Few Words About Cloth Diapers

Let's just say there are plenty of plumbers who put their kids through college thanks to stopped-up toilets from cloth diapers.

I totally get the valid concerns about disposable diapers clogging up landfills. But remember: all the loads you'll have to wash and dry impact the environment, too. As for cleaning . . .

So, if you want to use cloth diapers, go for it. I tip my hat to you. Just know you are adding another layer of stress to your life, along with a checklist of how to manage them: more frequent changes, less absorbability, leaks, rubber covers, safety pins. And you'll still need disposables whenever you're going outside with the baby. Many of my moms used up the diapers from the hospital, switched to cloth diapers, realized what a hassle they were, and said, "Oh, no, hell no. Sign me up for Pampers!"

I do love cloth diapers for two special reasons: first, they make the very best burp cloths. You can buy them in a twelve-pack, and you can never have enough. They're really soft and get softer with each washing, and are just the right size for your shoulder. The second reason is they make great loveys. Many of my babies use them as their security blankets—meaning you can quickly replace them because you have an identical stash in the closet.

Wipes

The closest you can get to water is best—an old-school, soft, wet washcloth is actually best. Warm water is really all you need. This is great when you're at home but not very convenient when you're out, so that's when you should use fragrance-free, water-based wipes.

This is a good time to train yourself to put on your reading glasses and check those labels. No matter how well known or expensive the item is, scour the list of ingredients and know what they are so you don't find your baby with an unexplainable rash that could have come from any number of products. (The only solution is an elimination test, reintroducing what you've used, one item at a time, and it's a real pain.) Some wipes have so much detergent in them that when you squeeze them, suds come out. Avoid those. You don't want any soap, chemicals, or fragrances that will leave a residue on your child's butt, causing irritation and diaper rash.

Even water wipes are not 100 percent water. Your little one can develop a sensitivity to them as well. You should occasionally use warm soapy water to clean their little bums. Save yourself the aggravation and use only the gentlest, most basic items for your baby.

Diaper Creams

A clean butt is your first defense, and zinc is your second. Zinc is the best diaper cream, which is why Boudreaux's Butt Paste is my tried-and-true, 200 percent, ride-or-die cream since forever.

One tube can last a whole year. It does not mask the skin but absorbs right in. It's not greasy or smelly, it's easy to apply, and it doesn't stain your clothes—everything you want in a great diaper cream.

In the beginning, diaper cream should be applied after every diaper change—especially after every poop. When applying, only use a very small amount on the tip of your finger. For a diaper rash, just use a little more cream. You don't need to slather it on like you're buttering bread!

Lotions and Powder

Shea Butter

Organic shea butter is my go-to lotion. It is hypoallergenic, completely inert, and unscented, so it won't cause irritation. It is also very economical—a little goes a very long way. It's wonderful for all kinds of irritations, and you can use it on your face and hands, too. If it's too thick, simply roll it around in your hand until it softens.

Other Oils

Other purely organic oils, such as jojoba, avocado, or vitamin E, work well, too. Whatever you choose, stay away from anything with fragrance. I never wear perfume when I'm working with babies because fragrance is a known irritant, especially to infants' sensitive skin. Besides, your baby has the best natural smell in the whole world. You don't need to put on anything to mask it!

Baby Powder

No baby powder. Period! That was easy! Talc can cause respiratory problems, and your baby will be just fine if you use a nice warm washcloth and butt paste.

Cleaning and Bath Products

Simple choice: organic and fragrance-free. Look at the labels—if there are a lot of chemicals, choose something else. Avoid shampoo with sulfates, as these are harsh detergents that cause lather. Sulfates are great for cleaning your car—not your baby's tender head! For more about bathing, see p.143 in chapter 7.

Pacifiers

The best choice for a pacifier is the old-school model with the brown nipple, now called an organic pacifier. It feels like rubber, but it's not hard and will get softer as the baby sucks on it. A pacifier should fill up the void in a baby's mouth, just as the areola does in breast-feeding. This pacifier is not synthetic and feels more human-like, mimicking the feeling of a nipple.

+ Avoid clear or white hard plastic. The pacifier should be soft.

+ Try different pacifiers before you determine the baby doesn't like them.

+ You'll need at least six pacifiers that can be sterilized and rotated. They should always be as clean as possible.

+ Always keep two pacifiers in your diaper bag, in case you drop one.

+ Pacifiers are to be used for extreme circumstances and sleep only. Don't diminish the power of the pacifier with constant use. See p.156 in chapter 8 for more on pacifiers.

FEEDING SUPPLIES

Baby Bottles

Even if you're planning to breast-feed, you'll need bottles for ex-pressing (pumping) your milk and for break feeding (allowing oth-ers to feed so you can rest). Plus, you also want your partner to do some of the feedings so you can nap and they can bond with the little angel!

It's All About the Nipple

The nipple is much more important than the bottle itself. A bottle's nipple has the same importance as a breast-feeding mom's nipple because it's all about the baby's latch, which should be a large one. This is also the key to having your baby be able to switch back and forth from nipple to Mom. Once you're past that hurdle, everything is so much easier.

A good nipple is soft and elastic. It should not become gummy or stick to itself when you wash it or become worn down or stretched out quickly—that will create a huge issue with gas.

A lot of my babies like to use the Dr. Brown's bottle. I don't have any particular preference—it's all in how you hold the bottle and keep milk in the nipple.

Glass vs. Plastic

Like so many generations of babies, I was raised on glass bottles and used glass bottles with my daughter. I realized what a pain they were when the miracle of the plastic bottle arrived. It didn't break if dropped, wasn't heavy, and if you warmed it, you didn't have to worry about third-degree burns on you or the baby.

But then we learned that all plastics were not made equal; re-

searchers realized bad ones were made from plastics that contained the chemical BPA, which is an endocrine disrupter that
mimics the natural female sex hormone, estradiol. In 2012, BPA
was banned for use in all bottles and sippy cups sold in the USA,
so the newest models won't contain it. They're hard and durable,
and you don't have to worry about throwing them out and hurting
the environment. Still, if you can smell the bottle and have an
issue with it, I would toss it.

For safety and insurance during travel, I'm a plastic person. If
you're out with the baby and the milk or formula is in a glass bottle
and you break it, you're done. Always use plastic bottles whenever
you go out. Even the glass bottles with silicone sleeves run the risk
of chipping.

Whichever bottle you choose, make sure it fits comfortably in
your hand, and remember—it's all about the nipple!

Bottle Cleaning

The soap you use for washing the bottles is more important than
the bottle itself. It can really make your baby miserable, or even
sick. Like many, I used to be an advocate for antibacterial soaps,
and then Dapple appeared in my life. It's the cleanest product I
have found on the market, and it doesn't absorb into the rubber
of your nipples or leave any aftertaste for your newborn. Dapple is
made purposefully as a safe cleaner for baby bottles, as it has less
cleansing agents and chemicals that could be harmful to an infant.

Whatever soap you use, make sure to rinse all your baby products very thoroughly. Even when you're sure you've done a thorough job, rinse again. A baby can't tell you when something tastes
different, so you need to pay close attention to those suds.

Also: No five-second rule for your newborn. There will be
plenty of time for them to put everything on the ground into their

gummy little mouths when they're teething, but for now, as soon as anything goes in their mouth and hits the floor it should be submerged in hot, soapy water followed by a long, hot rinse.

Burp Cloths

Burp cloths are your second skin and a safety net for anyone holding the baby. Baby skin is extremely sensitive, so you don't want to put them on anyone wearing any kind of fabric that could be irritating. If I had a dollar for the number of times I've had parents and grandparents politely tell me there was no need for them to have a burp cloth because they didn't mind a little spit-up. I politely explain to them it's not about them—it's about protecting my baby! Fragrance and fabric can irritate your baby's skin, so don't chance it.

As you know already, the best burp cloths are cloth diapers. Wash them in a very mild, unscented detergent. Always keep them washed and handy in case visitors covered in cat hair come over— you won't have to worry where they've been!

Nursing Bras

As a breast-feeding mother, you're going to be at your perkiest ever. Some days, in fact, your breasts will be so perky that you'll feel like you don't even need a bra—ignore that feeling. First-time moms might think of it as an investment, but all you second-time moms already know what I'm talking about!

You'll need at least four nursing bras: two for everyday wear and two for sleeping. It's hard to know your size before the baby is born, as your breasts will get larger when you're feeding, so ask a bra expert for advice. Anything that gives you easy access with one arm or one hand and that you can quickly unlatch and open will help you get ready for the feed. Try on as many as you need to see how they feel and work. You need to master your bras before going out in public. Try wearing a shirt with Velcro or snaps instead of buttons, which will be so much easier to open and close.

Remember to wash all your clothing, including your nursing bra, in the baby's detergent. Pretty much anything that comes into contact with the baby should be washed in their detergent.

How to Prevent Leaks from Showing

Nursing pads will be your safety net. Make sure you change them often and wear dark-colored shirts when you know you're going to be out for an extended period of time. Always keep backup nursing pads on you and an extra shirt if possible, and don't push the envelope between pumping or feeding sessions.

How to Cover Yourself for Privacy When Breast-feeding in Public

There are many options for privacy today that cover only the shoulder, breast, and baby so you don't have to play hide-and-seek. These covers are both practical and adorable. If adorable is not your cup of tea, I am sure you can find skulls and camouflage patterns as well. They come as scarves, aprons, slings, capes, or ponchos. They're lightweight and super easy to use. Practice using them at home so you can quickly whip them out when you're out with the baby and be all settled before your space is invaded by those who don't have a clear understanding of personal space, or as I would call them, Ms. How Come and What For.

Choosing the Right Pump

Depending on your health insurance, the hospital might provide you with a pumping kit, but if you have another preference, you can buy one at a baby store. It's better to use the hospital-grade pump, which makes pumping a lot smoother. Some store-bought pumps can leave you with sore breasts and pinched nipples.

Your breast pump is going to be your BFF, so get one that feels comfortable and is easy to use. You have to be completely familiar and at ease with assembling and disassembling it because it needs to be cleaned, dried, and put back together after every single use so that you are not looking for pieces prior to your next feeding.

There are both electric and manual models. Some are designed to pump both breasts at once, which makes them very time-efficient. A hospital-grade pump is expensive but also the quickest and quietest and can often be rented. (Pumps are considered medical devices; some are covered by insurance, but most aren't.) The electric ones work well, but make sure yours has a battery option because you might not always be near an outlet. If you travel a lot with your pump, look for a model that is lightweight and quiet. Though you won't know what level of suction will be the most comfortable until you're using the pump.

Spectra and Symphony are my pumps of choice. They are both high-end pumps, but choosing one is like choosing between a Mercedes and a BMW. Spectra is the newest on the market, but since Symphony has been around longer, it has a little more diversity (such as the travel pump). The great thing about both is that most of their parts are interchangeable between each other.

Although these are my top two picks, you should find one that you are comfortable with. Most women feel breast-feeding is invasive, so it is important to find a pump that is efficient and meets your needs. You can also seek help from a friend or family member who has used the pump you are using or speak to a lactation consultant. Fortunately, you can also YouTube the brand you choose and watch instructional videos.

BABY SAFETY

This is one area where advanced preparation is not only a must, but also a lifesaver.

CPR Training

Current CPR training should be required for everyone who will be taking care of your baby, as standards change quite frequently.

There are several options for certification. You can take classes as a group at home with a certified CPR instructor, which is great for those with busy schedules. You can also check with your local Red Cross center or organizations such as the YMCA for ongoing, on-site classes or even online options. No excuses. You'll be amazed at how reassured you'll feel with this training under your belt.

Baby-proofing Your Home

Baby-proofing your home should start before your baby is born. Although you won't have to clear the floors until your baby is old enough to crawl—babies are ninja-fast when it comes to putting something that looks like a defective science experiment in their mouths!—you will likely need to make some changes in what you have in your home and what you use to clean. A catastrophe can happen faster than striking a match, though it will feel like an eternity from the time it took place.

You will never forgive yourself if something goes wrong, so be mindful and start practicing before the baby is born so your new habits will stay with you for a lifetime.

+ As I said earlier in this chapter, clear your clutter before the baby comes home. Get rid of everything you don't need. Be ruthless. If you don't use it, give it to someone who can, or sell it. You're getting your nest ready, and that means having a clean, uncluttered house as well as a clean mind to see clearly down the road.

Clutter-clearing is so important because babies need a lot of stuff—you'll be shocked at how much space diapers, wipes, and other essentials take up. Plus, your friends and family will be bringing toys, gifts, and knickknacks that you have to keep because you know your mother, great-aunt, or mother-in-law will show up and ask about whatever they have made or bought Baby. Remember you have to play chess, not checkers, here. Save yourself by taking a picture of your baby in the outfit and sending it to them—just like that you've made a Bobby Fischer chess move.

✦ Secure everything within your home. Place all chemicals in your laundry room or another secure area (like the garage), store them up high, and lock the storage area. No toxic product in your home should ever be at baby- or child-reaching level.

✦ Change your cleaning products. If you use a lot of chemicals or bleach to wash your floors, your baby is going to be putting their hands on these chemicals as soon as they start crawling. Use nontoxic, organic, natural-oil-based products only. They work just as well as, if not better than, chemicals.

✦ Take your shoes off. Place a shoe box by the door, preferably outside if you don't have a mud room, because your baby can crawl over to it. The floor is your baby's play yard, and your shoes are going to track in whatever you walked on outside (which I don't even want to think about!). Instead of wearing your shoes in the house, change into slippers, moccasins, or any kind of soft shoe or socks with treads on the bottom so you don't slip.

My great-grandmother used to sweep the dirt on her outside porch. I know it sounds crazy, but she knew what she was doing. As kids, our laugh for the day was seeing her outside sweeping the dirt. But now, I see there was a lot of wisdom to having that broom outside the door. It actually minimized the dirt we would bring into the house.

chapter two

YOUR VERY OWN
MARY POPPINS

Getting Your Schedule Ready for Baby

Periodically Jessica Alba, a very excited and soon-to-be new mom, would visit her friend, news anchor Lauren Whitesell, who was also a dear friend of mine. She would come for a friendly chat and see everything I'd done to help Lauren with baby Ella. Lauren casually tried to tell Jess she would probably need a baby nurse, too. Jess gave that big smile and said very softly she thought she and Cash had it covered. Lauren and I looked at each other, as I said under my breath, "Bless your little heart."

Now, this went on for several more visits. Then about two weeks before Miss Honor's debut, Jess's whole thought process changed. She had that nine-month itch most moms get—let's just say they are ready for it all to be over! Jess began asking me questions about getting help and how to go about it.

Once Honor was born, reality hit Jess and Cash, and I received a phone call, Jess's little sweet voice trying to keep it together while asking for help. I headed her way, and though it was short and sweet, since I was booked for the Damons, she's still my baby!

Every parent deserves an extra pair of hands. Whether it's for a few hours, a few days, or a few weeks, a babysitter will give you some much-needed time for yourself. This person will become your saving grace and help you keep your sanity. If done right, having a helper can be the best experience in any new parent's life. It takes a village to raise a baby, but if you don't have that, then a baby nurse is your next best thing.

Now don't get me wrong—most parents can't afford full-time, live-in help. A baby nurse is truly a luxury, so if you can afford one, make sure you take full advantage of her knowledge and wisdom. I like to joke that you should start saving for her salary the minute you find out you're pregnant!

Most of my time with a family averages from three to six months. If you think you don't need to have someone for that long, or scheduling and/or costs are an issue, even a few weeks can be a tremendous help. It gives you a chance to get back on track and sort things out, especially with syncing your schedule with the baby's so you are all getting enough sleep and gaining confidence. Anyone who gives you the time to sleep is worth her weight in gold!

Finding the right person or day care takes time and energy. It's never too early to start the search—ideally, you're already on the prowl months before the baby is due. Ask all of your friends with kids for recommendations. If you are having trouble finding someone, child-care agencies usually have vetted nannies, baby nurses, and babysitters available on short notice.

CHECKLIST FOR ANY POTENTIAL CAREGIVER

Before you interview anyone, make a list of your wants and needs. Write down what your perfect nanny would do for you. Be brutally honest about your budget. There is no right way or wrong way—only what works for you. Remember, if you want professional help, act like a professional. Yes, hopefully this person will be a loving addition to your family, but you are still paying wages—this is a business!

I am a highly unusual nanny, as I've never worked under an agency. My three decades of work have all been through word of mouth, but even if you totally trust the people making recommendations, you should still have these questions answered to your satisfaction before making a decision. The questions will differ, obviously, based on the kind of help you need:

- What experience do you have?

- Have you had professional training/certification?

- How long did you work for your last family? How long do you work for most of your families? (This can vary, as I've had jobs that range from a few weeks to many months.)

- What were the best/worst things about your last few jobs?

- What was your typical schedule in your previous job?

- Do you have a flexible schedule?

- What is your preferred schedule?

- How do you get to work? Do you have trouble arriving on time? (Anyone with a long commute might be late due to traffic or public transportation issues.)

+ Are you willing to work overtime? Holidays? (Also cover your policy on sick days and vacation days.)

+ Are you okay with working for a three-month probationary period?

+ If you aren't an American citizen, is your paperwork in order?

+ Do you have children, and if so, how old are they? What will you do if your own children are sick?

+ Do you have a favorite age for the children you care for?

+ What would you do in an emergency?

+ How do you handle difficult situations, such as an inconsolable baby?

+ Have you had CPR and first aid training?

+ Do you have a water safety (swimming) certification?

+ Are you in good health and physically fit? (Taking care of babies and small children is physically demanding, and you need someone who can be as active as possible.)

+ Do you smoke?

+ Are you willing to be tested for illegal drugs?

+ Can you provide a recent physical?

+ Are you comfortable driving?

+ Are you comfortable with pets? (If applicable)

+ Who are your references? (These should be recent, with email addresses and phone numbers. Always, always check references before hiring someone!)

+ Are you willing to sign an NDA or a confidentiality agreement?

+ What are your social media handles?

+ What is your everyday uniform on the job?

+ Are you okay with being filmed with a nanny cam?

Last but not least, do a background check (including all married names, aliases, and states they've lived in prior) of the potential employee's driver's license, bankruptcy, and civil/criminal records.

PUT IT IN WRITING

If you are hiring someone for baby care outside of occasional babysitting, put all expectations in writing and make sure you pay them on the books. Any full-time employee working for you for longer than a week or two should have a contract. (If you're hiring someone from an agency, you should always have a contract.) This is to protect both of you. It makes clear your needs and prevents you from asking your employee to take on additional tasks (like housework) or work extra hours without pay.

Also, make sure your insurance covers anyone in your employ. Homeowners' policies usually do, but check to be sure. The last thing you need is for someone to have an accident while on the clock and need medical care that can bankrupt you.

DO YOU NEED A BABY NURSE?

Dee Dee Hoak, one of my moms who came through the Dallas network: "Nanny Connie swooped into our lives at the birth of two of our baby boys with her bag of tricks, filling our home with love, discipline, comfort, calm, and the *most heavenly smells of homemade fried chicken. Though she had to leave, she remains a hugely important part of our family. We are forever grateful for the gift of Nanny Connie. And, I hope the next book is a cookbook! I miss that fried chicken as much as I miss Nanny Connie!"*

Having a baby nurse can be the best experience in any new parent's life. Just a few weeks with a good baby nurse will take the edge off, and your inner psyche will calm down. I love seeing how all my parents instantly relax with me in the house, and having me around gave them a priceless opportunity for learning baby care without any stress. This made it so much easier for them to retain and be empowered by all that knowledge for the future.

The Baby Nurse's Schedule

Typically, a baby nurse will help you from ten days to three months, which is a perfect length of time, especially if you're breast-feeding.

I don't take days off, but I do take time off. For example, I tell all my families I go to church on Sunday mornings, so they can work that into their schedule. But I am prepared to be in the house 24/7 with the family. I know I will often be up for much of the night, so I take my deep sleeps during the day when the baby is with their parents and/or sleeping. Fortunately, with most of my families, I really feel at home.

My availability is not the industry standard, so be sure to arrange schedules from day one. Any baby nurse or nanny who comes in with their own schedule is a red flag; their job is to accommodate your schedule.

Don't Make the Night Nurse's Room Too Comfy!

A night nurse's shift is usually from around 11:00 p.m. to 7:00 a.m. She is there to ensure that you sleep as soundly as you would like and also to give you time in the morning to start your day before she leaves.

A night nurse does not usually require the amenities of a 24/7 baby nurse. All she really needs is a nice comfortable chair. I have heard of a night nurse being so comfy, however, that she slept as soundly as the parents. So, don't make your baby-care areas too relaxing in the beginning. You can switch to a cozier one once you're at ease with the night nurse or other caregiver and the baby's sleep habits are well-established.

Your Baby Nurse Is Part of the Family

Whether it's for one week or one year, your baby nurse is going to be living with you—and that makes her a part of your family.

I learned all about this kind of instant love for my families from Mu. She represented home and family and had a way of making everyone feel special and loved, the epitome of an awesome grandmother. Mu taught me how easy it is to soothe, calm, and connect with families on an intimate level. She also taught me that a baby nurse or nanny should always, always, have a relationship with all family members who come in and out of the house, especially other children. So, I help the mother deal with whatever she needs—in-laws, breast-feeding, eating, or sleeping; I help the dad by listening to his hopes and fears and discussing our shared interests; and I help the new siblings by playing and helping them understand this baby is here to stay. Sometimes it comes really easily, and sometimes it's really tough.

Personality is a must! I'm not saying your caregiver needs to be a chatterbox, but she needs to build a rapport with family members to smooth the way for everyone.

I was very young when I started as a baby nurse, and Huntsville, Alabama, was one of my hubs—it was close to home and gave me the opportunity to work while remaining within striking distance of my daughter.

I loved Julie and Harold Stevens and their three beautiful girls. Harper was their last child, and that's when I came into the picture. I would drive to Huntsville and pack all of the things I needed to stay over, including my rollers. I would roll my hair every night. The girls were fascinated, especially by how I could get the rollers to stay in my hair. Julie was also fascinated, and every night after she got the girls ready for bed and was feeding the baby, she would make me promise to wait before I rolled my hair so everyone could watch and wind down as I told them stories. It was such a great way to end the day, and it was perfect bonding time. My job wasn't just about the baby being happy; it was about the entire family being happy.

But as much as your baby nurse will love spending quality time with your family, you also need to make sure she has a room that gives her privacy during her time off.

I've been so blessed that my families have respected my space and respected me as a trained professional. I work twelve-hour shifts with no break and plan on pulling all-nighters, and that kind of job requires a certain level of respect from the parents who've hired me. A lack of respect is one of the quickest ways to burn a baby nurse or nanny out.

I make it clear that I am not a housekeeper or chef. My primary responsibility is to the baby. I help parents—emphasis on moms—learn how to care for the baby. That includes their personal care, nutrition, clothing, and even their toys. Now, there have been families I have gone above and beyond my immediate responsibilities for. That's because we formed a unique bond, and it was done out of my sincere love for them, not out of obligation.

But one family who approached me asked for my contract, and the father, a lawyer, reviewed it and made some revisions, which included me taking care of all the needs of the family, including cooking and cleaning. I would be promised a place to sleep and a bathroom. I quickly bridled my tongue—but I didn't bridle my thoughts—because obligating me to go above and beyond the scope of my job description is not an option. Needless to say, I passed on the job.

Don't make your nurse feel like a slave in the house. If she happens to want to take care of all the family's needs—cooking, laundry, housekeeping, and babysitting—in addition to her role as baby nurse, you need to catch the next flight to Vegas because lady luck is all over you!

DO NOT FEEL GUILTY IF YOU HIRE A BABY NURSE!

In many cultures, live-in helpers surround a new mother so she can regain her strength and get used to baby care. It's a sorry shame that Western countries try to make you feel that there's something wrong with you for asking for help. Don't fall for the okie-doke! You deserve all the help you can get.

No shame, please! Even if you've spent your life as a professional nanny and know everything about infant care, you need to get your strength back. You need time to adjust. You need to sleep.

I say this because some of my parents, especially my moms, are ashamed to tell me they slept well. Well, I'm pissed if you didn't sleep well. Hell, I've been up all night, so somebody in this house better have slept well!

NOT JUST THE HUNCH, FROM AMY THOMPSON

"I was blessed to have had Connie Simpson as a part of my life twice. There's no doubt in my mind she figuratively and literally held my hand, kept me Pamper-ing and pumping (Medela—our BFF), and overall soothed the home front. She's a baby whisperer, a husband whisperer, and one of my dearest friends. Few have had more of an impact on my life.

"When my last OB checkup broke the news that I didn't have the extra weekend before delivery that I'd planned, but would need to check into the hospital that very day, the first call I made wasn't to my husband. Panicked call number one was to the contractor finishing up a major renovation to include a new nursery. Panicked call number two was to Connie, smooth, calm Connie, the expectant mommy whisperer, at work.

"Connie's magic touch is so much more than getting a newborn on a schedule, making breast-feeding a success, and helping a new mom get some rest. She knows the secret to a happy new family is *the husband*. Getting Dad involved and adjusted and keeping him *fed!* Connie hauled out my great-grandmother's hundred-year-old cast-iron skillet and put it to work. Fried chicken soon overwhelmed even the sweet smell of baby Mustela lotion.

"Laughter. Connie brings it in spades. Plopping Mattie and Kathryn up on her chest after a feeding. Dressing up big sister to make her feel special. Taking trips to the hospital lab every other day to check my youngest's bilirubin—Connie made this chore a total hoot. Assuring me I needed a beer a day to keep my milk supply up. A new mom spends her days hunched over a changing table, a breast pump, or laundry. Connie took the hunch out of my first week, literally with her patented Mama Back Rub to get the knots out and figuratively with her laughter, common sense, stories, and unruffled warmth to get the mental knots out, too.

"I was truly mothering without a map as they said in those early days, without a strong mother relationship or example to follow. Connie offered the map. And I continue to follow it to this day. Just Be the Parent takes on fresh new meaning and reinforcement with every new year. What Would Connie Do? My mothering compass. And in all honesty, I believe my husband would marry her if he could. His gloom was as visible as the tears I shed when she walked out the door.

"This precious and wonderful soul will always be a part of our family—and a huge part of my heart!"

DO YOU NEED A NANNY?

Finding your super-spectacular Mary Poppins is like finding a diamond in the rough, but if your nanny is truly the right fit for your family, she will be worth every penny and any adjustments you may have to make.

I am a firm believer that parents need time for themselves, and whether a nanny is live-in or live-out, she will allow you this. She's there to reduce your stress and guilt, especially if you have to go back to work. She is there to assist you in keeping everyone on track—because your family is only as strong as its weakest link.

A live-in nanny is an enormous gift who requires a huge commitment, as she will become a member of the family. You'll both be getting to know each other, so expect ups and downs, as with any new relationship. This is a serious commitment for both of you, so you need to have a conversation regarding all aspects of this job, including both of your wishes and concerns.

In addition to the list at the beginning of this chapter, key questions to consider for in a live-in nanny are:

+ Will she be forthcoming and willing to communicate?

+ Will she be respectful of your space and your family rules?

+ Will you be respectful of her needs?

+ Will you give her the privacy she needs, especially on her downtime and days off?

+ Will you be able to pay for her health insurance, Social Security, and do other paperwork properly? (You'll want to speak to your accountant about all the financial paperwork necessary when you have a full-time household employee.)

With a live-out nanny, budget some training time before the baby is born. The nanny will be able to time the commute and get familiar with where you stash the diapers and the snacks, and you two can spend some baby-free time getting to know each other better. Take her shopping with you for baby gear and ask her for advice. If all she does is hold the cart, this is a good time to reconsider her as your nanny!

If she is finishing another job before she starts with you, have her come during dinnertime or on weekends, if possible. If she can't, crash-course her by having her come over at your most hectic times during the day. If she doesn't nail helping you by jumping in without being prompted, again reconsider. Seeing how well she makes decisions and competently executes them will make you both more confident about your routine and expectations.

DO YOU NEED DAY CARE?

Day care can be working parents' lifeline and salvation. But finding a great day care can be difficult, so don't beat yourself up during the vetting process if you're having trouble. Again, make a list of your wants, needs, and budget—the super-popular day care might not be right for you. It's all about what fits your family function. Use these tips:

+ It's never too early to look into day care. Waiting lists are longer than the Appalachian Trail. I know parents who started looking the minute they saw that pink line on the pregnancy stick.

+ This is not an area to skimp on. You get what you pay for, and you need to be careful in the selection process. I hate to tell you, but some day cares put on a nice front but view your child only as a dollar sign.

+ Try to find a central location that is convenient for you and any family members who'll do drop-offs or pick-ups. In the event of an emergency, you want to be able to get there quickly!

+ Hygiene is very important. The environment should be clean, even though babies make a lot of mess.

+ Drive-by visits to check out the neighborhood and walk-ins are a must, especially during nap times and mealtimes to see how the babies are treated and fed. Parents should always be welcomed. If visits aren't allowed, drive on by.

+ Ask about the caregiver turnover and the ratio of caregivers to babies.

+ A day care with a baby camera that allows you to see what's happening at any time of the day will stop you from panic-worrying that the baby fell out of the bassinet.

+ Don't be afraid to have a conversation with the staff. Always voice any concerns. You should be given prompt and clear-cut answers.

+ Once your baby starts at the day care, stop by often, at different times, to make sure the smiling face you left at 8:00 a.m. is still smiling a few hours later. If they're not, you need to figure out if they're having a bad day or if something else is up. Trust your instincts!

+ Don't be afraid to see if they comply with the standards of your state family and child protection agency.

+ See if there are any prior or pending investigations with the child-care center involving the state's Family and Child Protective Services.

The truth behind day cares is that no one really wants to send their child to one. Parents either look for the best, the least expensive, or a combination of both. But just because it's the best school and costs you a mortgage payment doesn't mean it's the right fit for your child. The bottom line is: this day care is responsible for your most valuable possession, and if the employees aren't showing you they understand that responsibility, they aren't a good fit.

The question that makes the rubber meet the road is: what are you willing to sacrifice? Even if you're in love with the day care you choose, always maintain a watchful eye.

DO YOU NEED A BABYSITTER?

Babysitters are there to watch your baby for a very short time, so for day-to-day care, they're a better option when your child is older and off to school. Your child will be potty trained, able to communicate if something is wrong, and old enough to enjoy playing with someone new. I suggest making a list of some eager high schoolers and college students (preferably pursuing degrees in early childhood education, social work, or even nursing), though I prefer the latter.

For now, though, a competent babysitter can be a tremendous help if you have more than one child who needs looking after or if you need to get errands done or spend time with your partner. Vet the sitter very carefully and give her a detailed list of your expectations so you can be confident your child is in safe hands when you go out.

If you have a son, don't be afraid to look for a manny (male nanny) or a male babysitter.

Don't always expect a family member to be your go-to babysitter. If there are any problems or unmet expectations, a strain on your relationship is the last thing you want or need!

CHOOSING A PEDIATRICIAN

Interview Different Pediatricians Before the Baby Is Born!

Finding the right pediatrician isn't always easy, especially if you live in a small town. So always, always start your search as soon as you find out you're pregnant. Write out your concerns before looking for your pediatrician. You should know:

+ If the doctor or practice takes your insurance

+ How quickly you can get an appointment

+ How quickly the doctor or practice responds to medical concerns

+ If the doctor(s) are good listeners

- ✦ Who is on-call after hours

- ✦ Hospital affiliations

- ✦ What the waiting room is like. Is there a well room and a separate sick room to isolate contagious patients? Is it clean?

- ✦ How close is parking

- ✦ Are there weekend hours

- ✦ Read online reviews of potential pediatricians you have either been referred to or looked up, and ask friends for honest advice. Your obstetrician should also be able to help.

- ✦ The most important thing is how well your baby responds to the pediatrician, and this is obviously impossible to predict. You can, however, get a good idea of bedside manners if you go with a friend and their baby to an appointment. If there are multiple doctors in the practice, try to interview more than one, because nine times out of ten, you will see someone different at some point.

Dealing with Your Health Insurance

Once you've chosen your pediatrician, make sure you know what benefits your health insurance covers and find out when you need to activate your baby's coverage. Medical care for babies is very expensive, especially with so many visits during the first year, so you don't want to pay out of pocket. Find out how your health plan defines "well baby" and "routine" visits, as well. Make sure to take all your insurance information to the pediatrician's office before the baby's first visit. All paperwork should be completed so you don't have to fill it in when you're sore from the delivery or with a crying newborn!

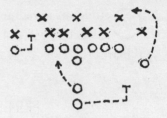

chapter three

HEAD IN THE GAME
Your Personal To-Do List

I love telling the story of Ms. Emily Blunt. She and I were friends long before little Miss Hazel arrived. We had such fun going over the list of everything she had to buy. She would give a little laugh at the names of stuff, not understanding what a Whoozit or a Boppy was.

Now, let's cut to when Miss Violet was just a nugget in the oven. Emily breezed through making her hospital list for Violet's arrival. I was so impressed that she was able to advise all of her pregnant friends on the things they did or didn't need. She even felt empowered to tell moms when they were going in the wrong direction. It was really funny to watch her in action and give her sweet British laugh at the end of the conversation. Then she would call me to make sure she gave the right advice or name of a product. I was so proud she had her head in the game. I can only say I tip my hat to her!

Getting organized and setting boundaries now are excellent habits that will make your life so much easier once the baby is born.

PRE-BIRTH CHECKLISTS

Your Children

Start telling children you already have about their new sibling once your body starts to transform. Describe as much as you want, in an age-appropriate way, about the birth process. Their little minds won't process it all, but they'll get the highlights. Put up a calendar and mark important dates; children work well with visuals.

You will need to line up a family member, friend, or babysitter to watch your kids during the birth. Once you go into labor, be honest about what's happening and when you should be coming home—with a new brother or sister. This is especially important for younger children.

Your Partner

Go on dates with your partner—for lunch, brunch, dinner, late-night snack, a walk to the beach, or any uninterrupted time together. It's so important that the two of you spend time together before the baby takes charge!

Your Immediate Family

Let individual family members know their roles (see more on p. 69), and don't be afraid to ensure they stay in their lane. You are creating your own family, and that's your priority.

Set boundaries and delegate duties so no one is stepping on anyone else's toes. Base task assignments on personalities and skill sets. Don't ask a Nervous Nancy to be in the delivery room with you—she'll either get on your last nerve or pass out when things get messy. You need to be as stress-free as possible while giving birth!

Pets

Your pet knows they were your first baby. They also know that something big is going on. You might have the most loving and adorable cat or dog in the world, but they might end up hating your baby. This doesn't happen often, but when it does, it's heartbreaking. Speak to your vet about helpful ways to transition your beloved pets into their new life with the baby.

Cats tend to be a problem more often than dogs do because they're very territorial, sneaky, and quiet. One time I went with Mom and Baby to the pediatrician, and the door to the baby's room was left open a crack. The cat got into the crib and tore up everything in it. As soon as I saw the damage, I told Mom the cat had to go, but she'd had him for many years and couldn't do it, even though I told her a cat can smother a baby—not so much from maliciousness but from smelling milk still on a baby's face. Cats can literally lick a baby to death: if they think the milk is coming from the baby's mouth, they can lick so much that the baby won't be able to breathe.

Dogs, on the other hand, are usually less territorial. You can hear them coming, and they don't normally jump up into a bassinet or crib. They don't usually interact with the newborn—or become an issue—until the baby is able to move around on the floor.

If you do have a pet, have your partner bring back a blanket from the hospital so they can get used to the smell of the baby.

Spend some extra quality time with your pet so they don't feel left out. Get them their favorite treats and ease them into the transition. Never assume you know what your animal is going to do. This is a new situation, and jealousy is real. My first rule of thumb with pets: Don't leave your baby unattended with your animal. Ever.

That said, pets and babies can have an amazing bond, and teaching your baby to respect an animal will serve them well as they grow older. Don't be afraid to get your vet's advice on ways to help with the transition.

Birth Announcements

This is an ever-evolving art. Announcements that were once mailed are now posted online. If you plan to go about this the old-fashioned way, gather addresses and rank them in order, from the most important (must receive immediately) to "forget about it." Prep your mailing list prior to your baby's birth, and try to send out birth announcements within the first ten days of Baby's arrival. Also try to send any announcements going to the elderly or more traditionally minded in your first batch. Trust me, they will wait every day until they receive that announcement!

Pregnancy Photos

I highly recommend you take them to document this miracle. One of my biggest regrets is that I don't have any photos of me while pregnant. Trust that you will definitely want to remember the journey even if you can't see your feet now and have enough gas to drive cross-country! And later on, you will want photos when talking with your kids or sharing priceless memories with your grandkids. My daughter is thirty-five years old, and I am still thinking about it!

I suggest taking a mix of candid and professionally staged shots to make sure you capture how beautiful you are during your pregnancy.

TO-DO: GROCERIES, SUPPLIES, PRESCRIPTIONS

+ Four weeks out, stock up on your staples. Clean out the freezer; if you're going to be breast-feeding, you'll be storing extra milk and need all the space you can get!

+ Take the time to write a complete grocery list for at least two weeks. Attach simple recipes to it so anyone who comes over to help can whip up your favorite dishes. Put it somewhere in the kitchen where it can be seen easily, such as on the refrigerator.

+ In any spare time, try to cook some of your favorite meals that can be frozen.

+ Petty cash is always good to have when approaching your delivery date. It doesn't have to be a staggering amount, but enough for someone to make a quick run to the store when you run out of formula or need some more butter.

+ If you plan to breast-feed, be mindful of gassy foods and leftovers that are more than forty-eight hours old. Stay away from broccoli and cabbage, wean yourself off of caffeine, and avoid chocolate and nuts. The less gas you have in your system now, the less gas your breast milk will produce in Baby.

+ If you already have a little one, be sure to stock up on their needs. Buy extra snacks, diapers, formula, and/or milk for at least two weeks, so you don't have to think about it.

+ Refill any prescriptions prior to the baby's birth. You don't want to be staggering bleary-eyed to the drugstore when you've got a cranky newborn!

YOUR BIRTHING PLAN

If you are planning on a hospital birth, read on for my hospital advice. If you're planning on a home birth, I'm sure you know by now that you need to make contingency plans to go to the hospital, just in case.

Checklist for All Births

No matter where you have your baby, a basic birthing plan should include:

+ Easily accessible contact information. This should include your doctor and important family members.

+ Packed hospital bag kept either in the car or by the door.

+ Extra sets of car keys and house keys.

+ Grocery list for two weeks after you come home.

+ Schedule for any children you have.

+ Schedule for any pets you have.

+ A basic home birthing plan should also include where your birthing area is—somewhere that makes you feel as comfortable as possible and normally includes an element of water (tub or birthing pool) and lots of towels on hand.

This information should be as detailed as possible. Nothing is too small to overlook (where the tea bags are stored or how to turn on your vacuum cleaner and washing machine). You want to make this transition as easy and as stress-free as possible for everyone.

Hospital Deliveries

Expect the unexpected. You can make all the plans you want, but your baby runs the show. You should:

+ Plan the atmosphere of your room (music, scents, favorite cup, etc.).

+ Discuss all potential scenarios that can arise during labor and have a plan for how you want to proceed in each.

+ Review your full plan with your obstetrician, and put the plan in writing so your partner and any other family members are aware of your wishes. This is crucial in the event that you're unable to discuss anything due to a medical emergency during the birth (such as an unplanned C-section), or if your obstetrician is not available when you go into labor.

+ Talk to your insurance company and be sure your paperwork is in order. Everyone who treats you needs to be covered by your insurance network.

Packing Your Hospital Bag

Take only what you need!

+ Toiletries

+ Hair-care products

+ Nursing bra

+ Comfortable clothing to wear home (elastic waist or loose-fitting dress)

+ Two to three nightgowns

+ Sanitary pads

+ Two to three pairs of socks and underwear

+ Journal and pens

+ Baby book (so the baby's footprints can be documented)

+ All medications you are currently taking

+ Soft clothes for the baby to wear home (make sure they are washed)

+ Diapers

+ Written birth plan

+ Delivery call list

Also make sure you have the appropriate infant carrier installed in your car—they won't allow you to take home your baby without it. Secure any other car seat as well.

If you live in a metropolitan area where you use a car service, most hospitals will still require the car seat to be safely installed for the car ride home. You will need to bring the infant carrier to the hospital, as they will not by law let you leave the hospital without the infant carrier being secure. Make sure you inform the car service that you will need to safely secure the infant carrier once they arrive at the hospital to pick you up.

Who Can Be There

The best-case scenario is to have the first row of your peanut gallery (grandparents, aunts, and uncles) in the waiting room. Not everyone needs to pile into the delivery room with you. The birthing area is for you, your partner, and essential family members you are comfortable with. The waiting room, on the other hand, can be filled with as many people as you like.

This is your time. After you and your partner have had the initial welcoming of your new bundle of joy, allow the peanut gallery to take a peek at the baby in the nursery while you are resting.

EVERYTHING WILL BE FINE, FROM STEPHEN BRODSKY

Just to set the tone, there have been two terrifying days in my life: the day our twin boys entered our home and the day Nanny Connie left it. This is what happened in between. How do you describe Connie Simpson? Some will no doubt compare her to Mary Poppins, and, in a sense, I suppose that is true. When I picked her up at the airport, she certainly appeared that way to me. She didn't have an umbrella or anything, but she did arrive carrying only a small bag—one that somehow contained everything you could possibly need. Even then, you could tell that Connie had accumulated the wisdom of someone who'd navigated every issue known to a child. Most important, though, she took charge of a situation that, for me at least, had spun out of control.

My wife suffered complications soon after the delivery, running a high fever that the doctors seemed unable to control or properly diagnose. It was a scary time. Thankfully, she would recover, but not before many sleepless hospital nights. Soon the boys would be released, and I spent the days shuttling between home and hospital, not feeling like much help at all. I struggled with where to spend my time. Everything had become zero-sum. At one point, Connie looked at me in the way only she could and said, "Don't worry. Everything will be fine." And you know what? I believed her. Remarkable when I think about it. Here was someone I'd only met a couple of days earlier. Someone I knew very little about. And yet, she put me immediately at ease. I've never seen anyone (before or since) manage a crisis so effortlessly.

All of which is to say that when the last morning of Connie's stay crept up on us and it was time for her to pack up that small bag and fly away, she very quickly diagnosed the fear in our eyes. "Don't worry," she said. "Everything will be fine."

Thanks to her, she was right.

Home Deliveries

Planning a home birth is a little more complex. You have to make sure your home is stocked and ready for the delivery—you can't run to the store in the middle of labor because you forgot something!

I can't stress enough how much you need to understand that home births can end up being hospital births. Hope for the best, prepare for the worst, and make a hospital plan just in case. This will prevent you from becoming scared or panicked during labor.

When the time comes, part of your plan will be delegating tasks to your helpers. This can be phone calls, moral support, ice-chip feeding, or driving you to the hospital. Line up your support system and make sure you have a daytime crew and a nighttime crew, because you're not going to have any control over when your labor starts.

Doulas and Midwives

A midwife is a trained and licensed medical professional who specializes in births. You absolutely cannot have a home birth without an experienced and certified midwife at your side during your entire labor. She should have already spent time with you going over the process—and being blunt about pros and cons. You should feel comfortable with her and trust her expertise. And part of this expertise, of course, will be knowing when to call an ambulance if you need to get to the hospital in a hurry.

A doula is a trained support professional there to assist and help you through the birth. She may or may not have medical training in obstetrics. Many moms love having a doula on hand for moral and physical support, as the doula is trained to remain calm and gentle during birth. She should also have a wealth of information about all aspects of the birth process.

In choosing a doula or midwife, you want to find someone you can see yourself building a relationship with. They should also be willing to provide their certifications and references. Speak with some of the parents they've worked with before. Don't be afraid to check on their certifications and be sure they can practice in your state. No question should be off-limits or thought of as "dumb." Your midwife and doula have your baby's life—and your life—in their hands.

FOLLOW MY LEAD

I have a lot of aunts who helped their sisters with their births. These aunts are wonderful and loving people, but many of them don't have children of their own—which never stopped them from having definitive ideas about baby care and child rearing. Sometimes this caused clashes.

I'm sure you can tell where I'm going with this! People with good intentions usually want to do things their way, and they often can't understand why their advice isn't heeded (or even wanted!).

This is why your new mantra needs to be Follow My Lead.

You are going to be the parent, so your lead is the lead to follow. Yes, you can ask for advice, but your baby is going to be raised your way. You are the one who's going to have to say, "Okay, thank you so much for telling me that, but this system works for me."

With the unspoken punch line being, "And don't you forget it!"

I am including this mantra pre-birth because you need to get ready to stand your ground. You are the parent, and this is your baby. You are in charge. It's your way or the highway.

I know stating your needs and expecting your lead to be followed can be difficult with certain family members, especially new grandparents. But let me be clear: if you don't stand up for yourself now, I guarantee you will be setting yourself up for problems in the future. Be clear and calm. No one is a mind reader, and helpful people are usually grateful to have rules spelled out for them. (Know-it-alls, on the other hand . . .) This could be as simple as having people take their shoes off before they set one little pinkie toe inside your home, or as complicated as figuring out who's allowed to spend more time taking care of your baby.

This is why I am upfront with parents about setting boundaries early on. All your loved ones need to know that it's *your* family, not *their* family.

part two

WHERE THE RUBBER
MEETS THE ROAD

The First Day of Forever

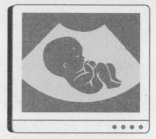

chapter four

JUST ONE MORE PUSH

Giving Birth

The day I went into labor, I was determined to watch the Cowboys and the Redskins play and eat my mom's turnip greens and cornbread dumplings—that's some good eating—before heading to the hospital. Turns out, that was a pretty good deal because my labor lasted twenty-two hours from my first nibble until they broke my water . . . then I came to find out nothing is done until you reach 4 centimeters of dilation. (Your cervix needs to be dilated to 10 centimeters before you can begin to push out the baby.)

Imagine being in a holding pattern with no epidural when dilated to only 3 centimeters. It's called hell on earth. But then the glory of the Good Lord shines through and you finally get to 4 centimeters. (Getting an epidural earlier might slow down your contractions.) Now, here is where it can get tricky. You have waited so long for that glorious epidural that will not let you feel any pain from your waist down, and you've reached that magical 4-centimeter threshold. But now things begin move pretty rapidly . . . and you may not even get to enjoy your epidural. Hold up, I will say it for you: *DAMN, DAMN, DAMN.*

But if you should get to the happy Land of Epidural, you will feel so empowered. You feel no pain, as if you could push forever. Then you hear the last thing you want to hear—"We may have to do a C-section"—and then you white-knuckle the side of the bed and say, "HELL NO, I'm going to do this!" Then you finally give in, and you move on to the C-section.

Nope, not me. I chose to white-knuckle the side of the bed and push because I was not going to be defeated. My daughter came out as a vaginal delivery, but my tailbone paid for it. Oh man, my episiotomy was not one to be desired.

Your body and the new infant have their own plans, and there is no failure in having a C-section. I am so grateful it is an option now. The recuperation can be, for lack of a better word, a bitch, but that beautiful little baby of yours makes it all worth it.

EXPECTATIONS FOR THE BIRTH

No two births are the same, be it at home or in the hospital. Collect all the information you can from your peanut gallery—your friends, coworkers, and family members who have had the privilege of giving birth—and then realize that no matter what the peanut gallery told you, you will do what you want in the end because you are on that delivery table, lying there as pains start shooting up through your butt, running up through your throat, coming up through your fingers, and shooting out of your ears! All your preparation can fly out of the window on the big day. Between the Good Lord and that infant, you will quickly learn you have no control—and that is only the beginning.

Some moms vividly remember every moment of their delivery

because of their rapid dilation and even-more-rapid blissful rapture when that epidural hit. These women are part of a very unique club, and we can't hate them.

So much of birth depends on the size of the baby's head, how much they weigh, how their shoulders come out, and how well your body responds to the contractions. I know moms whose very first baby was delivered easily after an hour of labor, no episiotomy needed. Then their second baby led to twenty-four hours of labor, eighteen stitches, and sheer exhaustion for days afterward.

What to Do When Your Water Breaks

A watched pot never boils. First-time moms can sit very patiently, but when that first labor pain hits, you will know it is time to move and move now.

When your water breaks—which is when the fluid in the amniotic sack leaks out—labor has begun, and you will know it! It can be a trickle or a gush and will feel as if you peed yourself, but warmer and more painful afterward.

It's time to call your obstetrician or midwife and follow their instructions. If you have a sudden-onset headache, racing pulse, abnormal swelling, or dizziness, call 911 immediately. Do not wait to try to reach your obstetrician or midwife. You might have preeclampsia, which is dangerously high blood pressure that can have severe consequences (although most cases are diagnosed during pregnancy; it ends with delivery of the baby).

Some women already feel contractions before their water breaks; it's unpredictable. If you do get to the hospital and are having contractions but your water still hasn't broken, have no fear. The nurse in labor and delivery will be happy to just pop that water right open and get things started. I had the pleasure of having my water broken, and, oh, the joy! (Brace yourself; it can be excruciating.)

THE JOYS OF BODILY FLUIDS

Giving birth is a messy business. It felt like every fluid inside me gushed out during the birth, and you lose all of your dignity because you have no control over any part of it. It's hard not to be embarrassed when you unexpectedly poop while you're pushing out the baby. (I bet the peanut gallery left that out of their birth story!) Don't stress. Literally, shit happens. It happens all the time, and the nurses take it all in stride because they have seen it all before.

The metamorphosis that your body will go through is indescribable, and the amount of blood and fluids you will lose during the birth is unbelievable. You will think there's no way in hell you can still be alive after all that, but you will! That's the miracle of giving birth.

YOUR FIRST GAZE AT YOUR NEWBORN

You can now heave a huge sigh of relief because your baby is here and you are okay. Many of you have seen childbirth on TV, and I am here to set the record straight: Babies you see on TV are not newborns. Most infants come out unrecognizable. This is more frequent in vaginal deliveries because of the journey through the birth canal. They are covered in vernix, a waxy substance that protects their skin in the womb. Their face gets squished, and they often emerge looking like one of the Coneheads from those old *Saturday Night Live* skits. The precious little infant just went through hell and back, so they have a right to be a little disheveled! This cone shape is absolutely normal and will correct itself within the first week. I have learned that cupping your *clean* hand and slowly stroking and molding the head periodically during the day will help with the shape. You can also alternate the position the baby sleeps in to help mold the head into a perfectly round little skull.

DON'T FEEL BAD IF YOUR BIRTH DOESN'T GO ACCORDING TO PLAN—MANY DON'T!

I've already drilled you about making birth plans, but don't feel like a failure if things don't go according to plan. Don't get so frustrated that you miss that glorious moment you've waited nine months for. Babies have their own plan of how they're going to come into the world. You just need to relax, be patient, enjoy the moment, and help the baby help you. Everything will be just fine.

Justin Timberlake and Jessica Biel: "Our story with Nanny Connie started the day we brought our son home from the hospital. That may sound like a normal statement coming from new parents, except our birth plan was anything but normal. We had two midwives, one doula, one meditation birthing class, a ton of hippie baby books, and a lovely home in the Hollywood Hills that we had turned into a labor training facility that we called The Octagon. So, not exactly normal.

"When all our plans fell apart and the serene, natural childbirth we had envisioned ended with a transfer to the hospital and an emergency C-section, we arrived home exhausted, disillusioned, and totally in shock. I was obsessed with everything organic, toxin-free, natural, and homeopathic for our kid, who came into this world in an operating room through an incision. I was a dictator, making myself and my husband insane!"

UMBILICAL CORD BLOOD

There is a hell of a lot of good in all that blood in the delivery room.

My first experience with storing cord blood was nearly nineteen years ago. The father took great care in finding out about the storage of the blood. I remember answering the phone after the birth of their first child and him relaying that the blood had been safely picked up and delivered to the cord-blood bank. I thought it was amazing and wondered why it wasn't always done as part of the delivery.

Fast-forward to now, and more and more parents are looking into and saving their baby's cord blood. It can be lifesaving for the baby, as well as the entire immediate family, down the road. It's used like bone marrow to help reestablish a healthy immune system, particularly with diseases like leukemia or sickle-cell anemia. Over the years it seems to have gotten a little less expensive to ship for storage at banks across the country.

Every parent should be given the opportunity to save something so valuable and natural. Do the research and see if it's a path you want to take.

Are You Really Going to Eat That Placenta?!

Caution: This conversation is not for the faint of heart! The placenta is the lifeline between the mother and the baby, providing oxygen to the developing fetus and allowing nutrient uptake and waste elimination. Once the baby is born, the placenta needs to be expelled in what is often referred to as the third stage of labor, almost like a second birth. The placenta usually comes out anywhere from twenty to thirty-five minutes after the baby is born in a vaginal birth. (It's removed with the baby during a C-section.)

If you think the delivery was messy, just wait until the placenta makes its arrival. Some parents totally lose it, and their mouths drop to the floor. A placenta looks like an alien creature. Google it if you don't believe me! It's got veins, it's lumpy, and it is bloody like nothing you've ever seen before. And that's okay!

The thought of eating something so massive that you discharged after birth sounds disgusting, but so many of my mothers have found a way to consume it. Most have it dried, so it can be placed into capsules and swallowed.

The supposed benefits are an increase in energy and output of breast milk, as well as a rebalancing of hormones. I haven't witnessed the benefits right away, but that is not to say they aren't happening subtly throughout the mother's body.

It's a good idea to speak with other mothers who have given birth and consumed their placenta, to see if it helped them. Doulas, midwives, and obstetricians are also great points of reference. This isn't foreign or taboo, so don't feel bad about asking questions.

Listen to me and listen to me good: This is your body and your choice. That's the only thing that counts. If you think consuming your placenta is a natural golden pill for increasing your breast milk or helping you with your hormones, honestly, there's no harm in trying.

If You Have a Preemie

There are thousands of blessings who come into this world and have to make a pit stop in the NICU (neonatal intensive care unit). Never underestimate any newborn's resiliency because when they need to, they rise up like little champions. Some of these babies have to be fed from syringes and eventually graduate to the red nipple for preemies. Once they find their stride, though, it's game on. They reach their fighting weight, all vitals check out, and they get to go home. I know one of the biggest worries about preemies is their ability to adjust and feed once you take them home, but time and time again I've seen preemies latch onto Mom like pros, which is always cause for jubilation.

Early on in my baby nurse career, one preemie family made me fall in love with my job even more. Not only was this a preemie birth, but it was a twin birth, too. They decided to make their debut around twenty weeks and stayed in the NICU for what felt like an eternity. The family lived about forty-five minutes from the hospital, and their mom would drive those forty-five minutes to bring her expressed breast milk around feeding time every day. I would be there waiting to help her with the twins and marveled at her devotion to her babies, Madeline and Morgan. She ensured her girls had the very best she had to offer. Seeing those little humans supported by all the tubes and monitors, in addition to all the special care the staff provided, made me step my game up even more.

Although the twins spent a nice chunk of time in the hospital, it didn't stop me from following my normal routine. The family and I would read, talk, and listen to music with the babies. These seemingly pointless activities were so important for their development and should be something all preemie families do daily. We could see the babies developing more and more through their responses to these activities. Helping those little miracles stay on track for all their milestones became my mission. We spent numerous days and months together as they matured from the red preemie nipples to the regular nipples most newborns are sent home with. We recorded everything from bottle ounces to baby weight to wet or soiled diaper weight. To see firsthand how I was making a positive impact in a circumstance as delicate as theirs brought me a joy I can't adequately express in words.

The requirements for preemies are really no different than those of any other newborn, but here are a few to keep in mind:

✦ Though it's not always the case, there is a higher probability that your preemie will develop at a slower pace than babies born closer to their due date. These developmental delays correlate to how premature your baby was. Always remember, though, there is absolutely nothing wrong with your little one—they just came early to the party.

✦ Clothing for premature babies should be kept warm, and those little skullcaps help tremendously in keeping them toasty.

✦ A premature baby is much more susceptible to germs, so keep visitors to a minimum. Make sure they wash their hands and have scent-free and debris-free clothing. It's your job to give your preemie a fighting chance to survive the encounter as germ-free as possible. This is especially important during the wintertime, prime cold and flu season. You should limit the traffic in your home even more and wash hands with soap and warm water—not sanitizer, and no, it doesn't count if you say you washed your hand a minute ago.

Bottom line: Having a preemie doesn't mean your world has come to an end. All it means is that you have to work a little harder at being a parent in those early stages. You got this!

HOW YOU'LL FEEL PHYSICALLY AFTER GIVING BIRTH

You've just gone through the battle of a lifetime. Don't underestimate how you'll be feeling—you need all the TLC you can get. Take your meds as prescribed, and don't be surprised if you start crying for no reason over the simplest little thing. Your hormones are going to be raging, and you and your partner should be very mindful of this. Both of you are still running on adrenaline, and rest is so needed.

HOW YOU'LL FEEL AFTER A VAGINAL DELIVERY

Limit Your Activity for the First Six Weeks

On average, your obstetrician will probably tell you to expect your vagina to be back to normal after about six weeks. Follow your doctor's instructions. I've found that most moms feel better a lot sooner than that, and I think doctors give you that extended window to keep your partner away—you know they can't wait to pay a visit to that area again, but they'll certainly stay away if your doctor tells them to. Patience is really a virtue here. Give yourself time to heal!

If You Had an Episiotomy

When I was told after hours of pushing with Courtney that they were going to have to do a C-section, I looked at my mom and told her I was going to push that baby out. Then I heard something like scissors cutting through a stack of paper, but it turned out the doctor was cutting my pocketbook (vagina) . . . Lawd, Have Mercy!

Episiotomies are the precise cuts made to your vagina so it doesn't tear when you're giving birth. However large the episiotomy needs to be, it is done in a controlled fashion by your obstetrician so it will heal more cleanly, whereas a tear can be extremely problematic to heal, as your vagina can rip all the way to your anus. (Sorry to be so graphic. You already know that giving birth is not for the squeamish!) If you do need an episiotomy, you are going to be very sore not just from the birth but also from the stitches in such a highly sensitive area. I hate to tell you this, but sometimes the stitching may not be right, and you'll have to go back in and have things restitched up.

These tips should help:

+ Sitting on a doughnut (available from medical supply stores or online) or a supportive cushion is amazing and will instantly relieve the pressure.

+ Take tepid baths with several handfuls of Epsom salts dissolved in the water.

+ Clean the area well whenever you go to the toilet. You will have to be very attentive to your lower half, and let me add one really good tip here: Plenty of Tucks pads are going to be beneficial in the healing of your bottom. They contain witch hazel, and every visit to the restroom should be used to help to heal your bottom. Plain old witch hazel is the best thing to use, and you can't use too much of it. It's an all-natural astringent that has anti-inflammatory properties, so it helps reduce swelling. You can also fill up a squirt or spray bottle with salt water or witch hazel and give yourself a few spritzes after you wipe.

+ Do not drive until you are totally healed. A hard head makes a soft ass! Any sudden movement between the brake and the gas can tear things apart quickly, so do not take any chances.

+ However sore you are now, you will heal from an episiotomy much more quickly than you will heal from a C-section.

How You'll Feel After a C-section

C-sections used to be the last, emergency-only resort for childbirth, but that has shifted in the last twenty years. For some women, especially those who are having multiples or are older, a C-section might be recommended to make the birth shorter and safer. For other moms, it's a deliberate choice. It can be scheduled on a day convenient for them and their surgeons, and babies plucked out via C-section certainly have less birth trauma than those born the old-fashioned way.

A C-section is major surgery. It is not a complicated surgery, but it is not a simple procedure either. Basically, all of your innards are pushed out of the way and piled up so the baby can be pulled out. I've heard many moms sitting around and talking about their birthing plans with their friends, discussing their upcoming C-sections—sometimes because they don't want to go through the pain of a vaginal birth—as if they were no more of a bother than getting a bikini wax. They're sure they're going to heal up really quickly. All I can say is: "Bless your heart!"

I've also seen many moms have unexpected C-sections, and they are unaware that this is major surgery. They are not clear on the recovery, the care, the scar that will never go away, or the immediate pain.

While C-sections are nothing to be afraid of, you are going to be in a lot of pain afterward. Your muscles will have been cut. You'll need to stay in the hospital for several days, sometimes longer if you had a difficult C-section or any complications. Expect your healing time to be about two weeks and pay very close attention to the instructions given to you and your partner when you leave the hospital.

You already read me say "a hard head makes a soft ass"—let me tell you here and now, I have many past C-section mamas who have baby-soft asses because they didn't listen. They thought these rules didn't apply to them:

✦ Don't lift anything weighing more than five pounds for the first two weeks. If your baby weighs more than that, you have to be very cautious if you do not have assistance. Don't try to finish the laundry or pick up your two-year-old in the saddle position. There is a reason doctors give you a lifting restriction of five pounds. Trust me, it will be hell to pay in the end.

✦ Don't consume spicy foods, sparkling water, or fizzy carbonated drinks, which cause gas and can be painful.

✦ Try to limit intense laughter, which can cause great pain. I remember being with John Krasinski and Emily Blunt right after the birth of their first baby. As a big Bernie Mac fan, John suggested we watch some of his standup. We didn't make it past the first two jokes because the laughter made Emily's pain so excruciating.

✦ Don't ignore the scar. Keep the area dry. This means no showers or baths until your doctor gives you the go-ahead. If there is any redness, unusual tenderness, swelling, or if you have a fever, call your doctor right away. You might have an infection that should be treated immediately.

✦ There are many over-the-counter creams to help scars heal, so ask your doctor for advice. Applying vitamin E oil or any neutral oil and massaging the scar will help the healing process once your stitches are out.

✦ Don't strain when you have to go to the bathroom. See if a stool softener will help.

✦ Don't run up and down the stairs. I can't begin to tell you the number of mothers who ignored this instruction, came home, ran up and down the stairs, and learned their lesson through the power of Mother Nature!

You see, life has a way of putting us in our place and making us listen. I have stood by many times, and the only thing I could say was "God bless." Some mothers just have to experience it themselves in order to listen, but I am trying to give you the answers to the test here!

chapter five

THE FIRST DAYS WITH BABY

Newborn Baby Bliss

Emily Blunt: I remember the first couple weeks home after Hazel was born. Emily was so happy. We were nestled in their country home away from prying eyes. This gave her the space and time to learn her new body. As with all my moms, I was happy to watch her as she settled into the reality of motherhood and began to heal her body—and she was just as content wearing her genie pants as I liked to call them. She didn't try on her pre-baby clothes in her closet for a couple of months, and I was so proud that she didn't put that pressure on herself. That mind-set allowed her to thoroughly relax. So, when Violet came along, Emily was prepared! My baby girl was playing chess, not checkers!

Y ou did it! There is no more amazing feeling in the world than seeing and holding your beautiful new arrival in your arms for the first time. Heaven!

Now the real fun (and hard work) starts. This is where you really learn about putting your big girl or boy pants on. It should be called the fourth trimester.

IN THE HOSPITAL

Breast-feeding

Your emotions will be running rampant from the delivery—you just went through one of the most physically and emotionally stressful experiences a human body can endure. And as soon as you catch your breath and realize you're really a mommy, you're expected to magically deal with something that is totally invasive and new and get that baby suckling like your nipple is the only thing in the world that ever mattered. Because, right now, to your baby, it is the only thing that matters!

Bless your heart! Everything will work out in the end. Some moms have babies with insta-latch, and some just don't. Some moms can pump only a teaspoon or two for a while before a good flow begins, and some can pump a half-gallon right off the bat. Don't let naysayers or any outside noise bother you or seep into your thoughts while you're on this journey. It takes awhile for the adrenaline that kept you going during the delivery to lower itself, and that can affect your breast milk. However much milk you start producing and however well your baby latches on, the most important thing is to relax. Being calm and relaxed is essential to milk flow—right after the birth and every time your baby feeds.

Let your brand-new baby be your guide. In all my years of helping moms breast-feed, there is nothing like watching a newborn get that apple-bite latch. Those little jaws are chomping away better than any pump I've ever seen. The baby ends up in a milk coma with milk running down the sides of their cheeks, gives me an enormous burp, and believe it or not, they are ready for Mom's other boob. You should aim to get them to do twenty minutes on each side. This doesn't have to be twenty minutes straight; you can break it up into five-minute sessions on each breast.

The first milk you produce right after birth is a clear fluid called *colostrum*. No drop of it is to be wasted, neglected, or wiped away, because it has more magical powers for your newborn than Tinker Bell ever dreamed of. It is loaded with crucial antibodies and a higher level of protein than regular milk, which makes it very important for your baby's health and growth. So even if your baby has trouble latching, or you plan to bottle-feed, make sure you pump out as much colostrum as you possibly can.

Patience and persistence will help your baby be a very efficient eater, and you will soon become a great milk mama! For more about breast-feeding, see chapter 6.

Visitors

Although you can invite as many people as you like during the birth process, as most of them will be in the waiting room and out of your hair, try to cut back after the birth. Yes, everyone you know will be thrilled and want to Instagram that baby right away, but I firmly believe visitors should be kept to a minimum. I always say: You will have enough visitors between your emotions and your new baby! This is especially true if you have a C-section. Once the anesthesia wears off, you will not want to have to deal with Aunt Josephine and Uncle John cooing over your precious little bundle when your insides are about to explode.

Remember, follow your lead. It's never too early to let everyone know that time and space will be very important when the baby arrives. Now is not the time to be shy.

Getting Ready to Leave the Hospital

Most doctors will follow up with you after the birth. Each hospital has certain criteria a new mother must meet prior to discharge—from making sure you can walk around to making sure you can poop. This depends on the hospital, physician, and insurance. Be sure to read the fine print on your health insurance policy, as they vary considerably about coverage for your postpartum stay. If you don't feel well when you're given the go-ahead to leave, say so! You know your body. Anything that strikes you as off should be reported ASAP, especially any fevers, excessive bleeding, or extreme pain.

TESTING THE BABY

Before the baby is released, they get a standard check required by the state. Each state has its own standards, ranging from hearing to pulse and breathing rates to reflexes.

A PKU (phenylketonuria) test is done to see if a newborn has the enzyme needed to use phenylalanine (an amino acid needed for normal growth and development) in their body, as well as to check for more than sixty other disorders. It's great to have, and it's usually required by your state. It can take on average three weeks to get test results back. PKU testing can be done within the first twenty-four hours after birth and repeated one to two weeks after birth. The best way to prepare for this is by warming the heel that will be pricked. You can rub it or place a sock or warm washcloth on the foot at least an hour before the blood draw to increase blood flow. It may take awhile, and if your baby is not a great bleeder, it can be very stressful for the parents.

All states mandate a bilirubin count (a liver assessment), which is also done with a prick on the heel for a blood sample. Don't be surprised if the level is a little high, as it's always elevated in a newborn. If there is anything at all wrong with your baby, they will always let you know right away.

Your little one may also receive the first dose of their Hepatitis B shots. Check with your physician to see what the protocol is for this immunization.

If you've had a boy and want him to be circumcised, this should be done before you leave the hospital. Most parents who want this procedure have already spoken to a pediatrician or pediatric urologist before the birth, but if you haven't done so, you'll usually end up with the on-call pediatrician.

If it's wintertime, some parents make sure they have the flu shot prior to leaving the hospital. Others want a hepatitis vaccine as well. Speak to your obstetrician to make sure everyone in your home has been vaccinated to their specifications.

When you're ready to leave, take everything that's not glued to the floor. I'm not kidding! Your room should be filled with samples of formula and diapers, and everything belongs to you once it's opened. If you don't have a lot of space at home and have a lot of flowers at the hospital, feel free to donate them to the nursery. The nurses will be happy to have them.

Make sure you eat a good meal before leaving the hospital and feed the baby as close to your departure time as possible, so you have two fewer things to worry about when you get home. It can be an outside meal or a hospital meal—just make sure you eat. Also, make sure any and all prescriptions are called in so they can be picked up while you're out.

Once you're done feeding, make sure to put on a fresh diaper. You never know when a simple thirty-minute car ride can turn into an hours-long nightmare.

BRINGING HOME BABY

The Car Ride Home

Before putting the baby in the car seat, I recommend giving them gas drops. Even a very new baby can suffer from a lot of painful gas. Nothing like a screaming baby to make the first car ride a memorable one!

I said this in chapter 1 and will say it again: Make sure you have tested the car seat prior to delivery. You need to be confident that you know how to operate it and that it's secure. Mom should ride in the backseat with the baby, so make sure it's as comfortable as possible. There should be water, snacks, pacifiers, and a burp cloth. If you're driving yourself home or using a car service, make sure you prepack those items in your hospital bag so it's one less thing you have to worry about.

Settling In at Home

I will be short and sweet here. The first day home is all about survival, and following your doctor's instruction to the letter. When you get home, this is not the time to try to be Superwoman. You have the next eighteen years to do that!

Moms: Take a pain pill, feed and change the baby, have a nice hot shower, then crawl into bed and go straight to sleep.

Partners: Do a quick run-through so your house is in order. Make sure all prescriptions are filled, all animals are sheltered, and remember, less traffic is best.

You must rest, so go ahead and put a quarantine sign on the door, unplug your phone from that charger, put your emails on automatic response to say you are out of the office, and close your eyelids. You have had a traumatic experience, and you need to come home and shut the world out.

The first twenty-four hours will be dictated by your baby. It's a good idea to try to maintain the schedule you had at the hospital, but it may not be realistic. Breast-feeding moms should expect to feed every two to three hours. Formula-feeding moms should expect to feed every three to four hours. On average, your baby will be sleeping according to their feeding schedule. You want to wake them every three hours or so to feed. (For much more about feeding schedules, see chapter 6.)

Start Keeping Your Feeding Journal on Day One

Keeping a journal of your little one's intake and output is essential for all parents. Even if you're too zonked to lift a pen, you need to crack open that feeding log on day one. If, like most new moms, you have Mommy Brain and can't even count to ten, it's incredibly easy to forget what time you took your meds, fed the baby, and other day-to-day operations. A journal will put your Mommy Brain back in order and build that confidence every parent needs. Get into this habit from day one, and it'll become part of your feeding routine before you know it.

It's important to log each feeding. Keep this journal near you at all times; you can even put it on your phone. In addition to writing it down, a good trick to remember what side you last fed on is by placing a safety pin on your bra after each feeding. If you don't alternate breasts, you won't necessarily dry up your milk, but your ducts won't produce the volume of milk you want them to. Your journal should list:

+ What side your baby ate on

+ What time the feeding started and ended

+ Wet diapers

+ Poop diapers

+ When your baby slept

+ When you slept

+ When you ate

+ How much water you drank

FOLLOW YOUR LEAD WITH VISITORS

Visiting Hours

Now that you're home and you've had some rest and good food, you can slowly start to invite over everyone you want to see. Do this slowly. Visitors can become very overwhelming very quickly.

No new parent should be caught off-guard by anything, especially visitors. I personally prefer no visitors at all for the first week (good luck with that!), but I'll settle for the first seventy-two hours, unless you ask visitors to get food or other supplies, keep you company, or provide support should your partner have to leave. This includes everyone from your parents to your preacher. Be sure to stagger the visits so you're not overwhelmed and you don't waste a good pair of helping hands.

Take advantage of all the help you can get, but not all at once. Use your help throughout the next few days and weeks to come, and stagger the visits.

New House Rules for Your Visitors

Once you've settled in, it's time to make new house rules for friends and family.

+ Do not call or text me after 7:00 in the evening unless it's an emergency.

+ Do not get mad at me if I don't get back to you right away.

+ Do not expect to spend a lot of time with the baby until they've had more of their shots.

+ Do not get offended if you're asked to cut your visit short due to nap time.

+ Do not get offended if I drop the ball with you—sleep deprivation is real!

Make sure everyone has a thorough understanding of your wishes, so they don't take them as light suggestions instead of requirements. My requirements include:

+ No perfume or cologne. Fragrance can be highly irritating to a baby who has spent the previous nine months safely protected in the womb and then all of a sudden is bombarded by some funky smells. As soon as I started working with babies, I stopped wearing perfume, and anyone helping you with your baby should, too. Besides, there's no more wonderful scent in the world than Eau de Baby.

+ No jewelry, which can scratch the baby.

+ *Absolutely no smoking* of any kind around the baby. If a loved one smokes, they have to go outside, as far away as possible from the baby, and then change their clothing before coming back into the house.

+ Everyone washes their hands before getting near the baby. I don't care if this person just wants to hold your baby's chubby little fingers for a second—you don't know where they've been, so those hands get scrubbed clean!

✦ Anyone with a cold or any bug must stay away. Your new-born's immune system is extremely fragile, and they are highly susceptible to germs.

✦ Hands off the baby's head. The soft spots are an open door to germs. Touching or rubbing the fontanels is like sticking their hand in the baby's mouth.

✦ If you find that the know-it-alls with their "helpful" advice are butting in before you've even gotten your episiotomy stitches out, use this handy phrase: "I didn't know that. Thank you." I say it all the time to purposefully make myself look dumb. I don't mind if it helps my new parents cope (especially when the in-laws are the "helpful" advice givers!). Sometimes it's much easier to nod, smile, and do the eye-roll in private rather than having a confrontation or getting upset that someone thinks you don't know what you're doing.

New House Rules for *You* and Your Partner

House rules aren't just for visitors! I can't stress enough how important it is to have nice, quiet downtime with your baby so you can get acquainted.

✦ At least twice a week, shut off electronics an hour before bedtime. This ensures time for an undistracted conversation, or if you're a single parent, time just to have a quiet moment with yourself so you can truly decompress.

✦ Slowly include more nutritious food in your diet. Junk food, especially if it's high in sugar, can cause false energy highs and lead to crashing lows, which will have an effect on your emotional highs and lows, as well as your ability to sleep.

✦ You need to have a routine. Trust me on this—anything you do now on a consistent basis (such as sleeping when the baby sleeps instead of posting photos on Facebook) will quickly become a good habit and help you stay on track. If you're the kind of person who's a little disorganized, as most people are, having structure is really hard. But the baby's schedule is invaluable. There is not a price tag you can put on your baby's schedule! Their needs have to be met—they must be fed and changed every few hours.

Don't beat yourself up if it takes some time to adjust your body and mind to this new routine. You are learning an incredible new skill set, and it takes time. It's all about that foundation. Build a strong and sturdy one from the minute you come home, and you're well on your way to raising a contented, thriving baby.

part three

OPERATION MANUAL; OR NO, YOU WILL NOT DROP THE BABY!

chapter six

FEEDING THE BABY

Brooke Shields: Sweet Brooke. Prior to going to helping her with her second baby, I remember saying my prayers that I would have all the tools to help her deal with the postpartum depression she had been so amazingly forthcoming about. No two pregnancies are the same, but I wanted to be locked and loaded, since I knew her prior experience and how easily postpartum can spin out of control.

Once Little Miss Grier arrived, I thought my focus would be on depression, but instead it turned to my familiar old friend: breast-feeding. Brooke had been so focused on postpartum her first time around that she didn't remember the amount of milk she produced or if she could even produce enough. I turned her bathroom into our pumping oasis. We had snacks, water, a cozy chair, and what became her favorite beer. There was so much laughter, joy, and relaxation in that bathroom. She could not believe the amount of milk she was pumping. There was enough milk to meet the needs of Baby Grier with plenty left to store. We bonded over beers and boobs!

GENERAL FEEDING GUIDELINES

How Often to Feed

Your feeding schedule in the first month is determined by how big your baby was at birth and whether your baby is breast-fed or formula-fed.

✦ Breast-feeding babies will need to feed *on demand*. This can be as often as every hour in the first day or two. Generally, in the first few weeks I advise moms to feed the baby on demand, but not to let the baby sleep more than three hours—four max—without a feed.

✦ Formula-fed babies will need to feed every three to four hours. That's because formula contains more nutrients than breast milk and is more slowly digested.

✦ A baby needs to reach a certain weight to sleep longer between feedings, so every pound at birth makes a difference. A five-pound baby will most likely wake more often than an eight-pound baby. Their sleep time will gradually lengthen as their weight increases. In addition, doctors have found that the frequency with which a breast-fed baby feeds typically depends on the baby and the storage capacity of Mom's breasts, which varies from one baby to the next. Yes, it is totally random.

✦ Write down when the feeding begins. Most moms write down the time when the feeding is done, but that will lead to confusion over the duration of sleeping and feeding and throw off the baby's schedule.

✦ If you let your baby sleep more than four hours in the daytime, they will cluster feed—or start eating every forty-five minutes to an hour—at night to make up the difference. The saying "Don't wake a sleeping baby" is only true at nighttime. (Although, I would still consider waking that baby at night, at least initially, if they're going more than four hours without a feeding.)

Nipples

Many parents don't know there are different-sized nipples for bottles. The nipple for the first two months is a #1, and for older babies, you should use a #2, which has two holes in it for a faster flow. It makes an incredible difference. A bigger baby can take more milk in, which fills them up faster and makes your feeding go more smoothly.

If you are a breast-feeding mother you will want to stay on a size #1 nipple until about three months, and then switch to a size #2. You don't want your baby to struggle when eating.

Pay attention when you first switch nipples because your baby may be overwhelmed with the flow of milk. Be patient and take your time. For whatever reason your infant may just not be ready to switch.

BREAST-FEEDING DOS AND DON'TS

Dos

Your breasts are now fulfilling their true purpose: pumping out liquid gold to support your newborn. Be proud and thrilled that your amazing body can do something this wonderful.

1   *Eat fatty foods!* You *have* to put fat in to get fat out for the baby. The fat in that fresh iced doughnut is going straight to your Krispy Kreme Dreams! Time to stock up on butter and

olive oil, too. Also, one of the best things to help with milk production is beer, believe it or not. A little beer doesn't have enough alcohol to harm the baby, but it really gets that milk flowing!

Jessica Biel: "What I learned from Nanny Connie is this: there's no such thing as too much butter when breast-feeding! Butter in oatmeal, butter in rice, butter on steak. Butter on skillet toast. Butter in coffee. Butter apparently cures. Turns out, it's also a crucial part of a child's brain development. Thanks, Nanny!

"And the meals she would cook for us. Whoo-wee. These meals that were for the production and maintenance of my milk fat, which I didn't know I needed to maintain. I was already having an issue with production, so I can't imagine what nightmare I would have been in without the advice she gave me—and all the beer she allowed me to drink!"

2 *Rest!!!* Especially during the first three weeks, which are vital for you and the baby. Minimize visits and socializing. Lie down when you want to. You just had a baby!

3 Sleep when the baby sleeps to minimize exhaustion. This also helps maintain your breast-feeding schedule so that you and the baby remain in sync. Your best milk comes in the morning because you've been inactive for a substantial amount of time, allowing the fat time to build in your breast milk—it's like Thanksgiving dinner to your baby.

4 Familiarize yourself with your pump as soon as possible. It will be your best friend!

Don'ts

1 Don't stress. Stress can and will stop milk production. You need to be as relaxed during this process as possible.

2 Don't sleep on your stomach. Sometimes breast compression can decrease milk supply. If you are a stomach sleeper and find your supply suffering, consider altering your sleep position to remove pressure from your breasts.

3 Don't skip your feeding log/journal. It is the only way to keep track of your baby's input and output.

BREAST-FEEDING 101: LATCHING ON

Now listen and listen good! No one said this would be easy. Hell, your baby may even draw blood. Yep, draw blood from a cracked nipple. Are you ready? Game on—let's do this!

Latching How-to

There is no particular breast you should start with. Babies tend to have their favorite one—normally the side they latch onto the easiest.

Picture taking a big bite out of an apple and the imprint left behind. That is what you should imagine happening to your breast—with no teeth (at least not yet). You want your baby's mouth to be that wide so they get full coverage of the areola.

Never allow the baby to just suck on your nipple. Not only should your baby not think of the breast as a pacifier, but also a nipple-suck will be unbearably painful for you.

Proper Latching

Sit wherever you're comfortable, and use as many pillows as you need. If you're not comfortable, it will make the entire process more difficult. I highly recommend using a feeding pillow (like a Boppy), which is horseshoe-shaped and specially designed to make your feeding easier. The horseshoe shape gives you 180-degree protection when feeding the baby, so that's one less thing for you to worry about. It also allows you to position the baby at a good angle on your breast.

Some are even textured to help keep the baby's head in place. My favorite is called My Breast Friend because it closes the gap between Baby and Mommy so that the baby does not get too comfortable and forgets the purpose of being in that position, which is to feed. (Not sleep!)

As I said, the success of a perfect latch is getting your baby to seemingly take a bite out of your areola instead of slurping the end of your nipple. To achieve the perfect bite, express some milk on your nipple. Assist your nipple to protrude by pinching your areola from top to bottom or side to side, and rub it beneath your baby's nose, bringing it just below the bottom of their lip. If you don't achieve a latch, express more milk on your nipple and run your areola corner-to-corner on the baby's mouth. Once the baby fully opens their mouth like they're about to take a bite of your boob, allow them to latch. You will feel long draws as if the baby is sucking a thick smoothie. Make sure you hold the breast until the baby has control of the boob, then let go and *relax*. They've got this!

What If My Baby Doesn't Latch?

Those first latches can be tough, and your nipples can become raw and red as your baby tries to suckle. Someday you will be able to laugh about this, but for now, you've got to try placing the baby on the nipple in as many positions as possible.

If the baby is not latching, they may be too comfortable or just not ready to eat. I can't tell you the number of times I have walked in on my mothers who have the "What do I do, I can't wake the baby" look on their faces. My response is, "Well, hell, I'd fall asleep too if you nuzzled me up like that."

A swaddled baby is a comfy baby, but that's not the way you should feed. Unwrap them and keep down-dressing them until they are totally naked except for their diaper. This allows air to circulate around the body to wake them up. I would also emphasize skin-to-skin contact here. When Baby smells Mom, they get hungry and know exactly what to do if Mom's shirt is off and the breast is out!

You can also tickle their feet, turn the temperature down in the room, or wipe them with a cold washcloth. A baby who's sleeping during a feeding is not going to get enough milk, and this will make it more difficult to maintain that all-important breast-feeding schedule.

"Tongue-Tied" Babies

While most latching issues have an easy cure that doesn't require a doctor's help, there are some situations that do.

The fold of skin beneath the tongue is called a *frenulum*, and it can tether the tongue (or lip) too tightly to the rest of the mouth. When this happens, the tongue (or lip) cannot move as needed to support a strong suckle. This is sometimes called "tongue-tied" and almost always comes with a lip tie as well. A tongue-tied baby can't suckle well, which often leads to slow weight gain and a drop in the mother's milk supply.

This is usually fixed by a procedure called *tongue evasion*, where the skin underneath the tongue is snipped to help the baby's tongue relax. It's done with surgical scissors or a laser, takes a mere few seconds, and heals very quickly. Most babies protest more from being held still for the procedure than they do from the actual clipping.

Some pediatricians don't pay much attention to ties, though— you might hear, "Well, if breast-feeding is painful or the baby isn't gaining, just use bottles or formula."

The real test is keeping up with the after-care. The skin can very easily grow back and then it will be all for nothing, which can be very heartbreaking.

Now, you may ask if it is all worth it. Well, I say this coin can be flipped heads or tails, and it's all in the preference of the parents. I have had parents who have done it and regretted it because they were so focused on the latch. Diligently do your homework, don't overthink it, and you'll come to the right decision for you.

When to Talk to a Lactation Consultant

Many women who have trouble with their babies latching on call a lactation consultant for help. Talking to a lactation consultant can sometimes be intimidating, daunting, and overwhelming. As in any profession, there are the good apples and then there are the bad apples, and I've experienced my share of the bad ones. Trust me, I have run into a few of those who thought the world revolved around their every word. It's like they come with their own little Bible and act as if their word is Gospel. But a good consultant can give you phenomenal tips on how to feed your baby. Just remember that not every piece of advice or scenario can be applied to your unique situation. You need to find a consultant who makes you feel confident and relaxed, because that will help you when the baby is hungry and the consultant isn't around to help.

Any lactation consultant who tells you that bottle feeding is wrong is not the one for you. There is nothing wrong with bottle feeding. Some babies just don't take to breast, for reasons un-known. Some moms have had surgery and can't produce milk. Some moms have such severe mastitis that they can't breast-feed. Guilt tripping helps no one. Certainly not you—and certainly not your baby!

Milk Production

Your most nutritious milk is produced between 4:00 a.m. and 9:00 a.m. You've had time to rest, which allows the fat to build up in your milk, so your girls are fully loaded and ready to go.

Your breast size has no bearing on your milk production. I've worked with moms who were as flat as a dime and thin as a sheet of paper, and they produced enough milk to feed triplets. Then there are those who put Dolly Parton to shame and can't produce enough to feed one baby. So, don't worry about your breasts. They'll be fine!

Those moms who have had surgery to enhance their beauty might have difficulty breast-feeding, though. In my experience, when my mothers believed the people who told her, "Oh, you can get implants done and still breast-feed," they have been sorely dis-appointed. I have seen too many mothers leaking milk out the back of the areola as opposed to their nipple or not able to put a dime's worth of milk in a bottle, much less feed a baby when pumping. This can be a very depressing moment for a mom, but again, do not think of this as failing your baby!

If, however, you haven't had implants or any other procedures on your breasts and still aren't producing enough milk for your baby, you should check with your lactation consultant or obstetrician.

No mom I know goes into breast-feeding saying she is going to produce the best milk ever. However, you do have to put your best foot forward, and that includes eating correctly, which means fatty foods. At this point, your waistline has zero priority. I'm not saying eat McDonald's Extra Value Meals 1–8, but hearty meals are necessary. This is a process and it isn't going to be easy, especially if you're a first-time mom, because you're teaching your body to do something it's never done before. You have to put enough calories in your system not only to nourish your child, but also to help yourself thrive.

Finally, water is key! Think about your milk ducts like powder formula. The only way you are going to turn that powder to liquid gold is by consuming gallons upon gallons of water. Tea, lemonade, soda, power drinks, or green juices are not options—I said H_2O!

If You Used a Surrogate

Using a surrogate is an emotional roller coaster. I'm sure you chose one who is loving, and finds great joy in being pregnant and bringing new life into the world. You should already know her medical history, eating habits, issues with pregnancy, and the level of your involvement while she's pregnant. Your surrogate is still your partner in this pregnancy. Even though she won't be raising your child, she will always be a part of the crucial process to get your child here.

If you are using your surrogate's breast milk, you need to be aware of her eating habits. It's hard to be a breast-feeding mother, and it's almost impossible to have a surrogate who may not even live in the state ship you breast milk, which can affect the viability of the breast milk. Also, issues like gas and upset stomachs can come up due to the surrogate's eating habits. I'm not saying it can't be done, but you need to have realistic expectations.

Cabbage Patch Time: Slowing Down and Stopping Milk Production

Are you ready to dry it up? Time to bind your girls!

Here's what you need: sports bras that are one size smaller, Ace bandages, ice packs, and cabbage leaves. Yes, cabbage!

Go to the store, get a big head of cabbage, and put it in the refrigerator so it's ice cold. Place a leaf directly on your boob in your bra, changing the leaves every thirty to forty-five minutes during the day. The salt content in cabbage is fantastic for drying milk production, and the cold helps with engorgement and swelling. This is the most painless method I know, and it really works!

A sports bra a size smaller helps tremendously with keeping the girls in check and eliminates any room for growth.

You will probably linger in this cabbage factory for around seven to ten days, until your breasts go back to their normal (or even smaller) size. At this point you can go back to one of the lovely lace bras in your drawer, because I know you want to get your sexy back!

How Do I Know the Baby Is Getting Enough Milk?

Your baby should be guzzling anywhere from four to six ounces per feeding, and you'll see a few signs.

After they have passed the meconium stool (the black-as-tar remains of what was inside their intestines while in utero), a breast-fed baby will average at least four to six stools a day. This should last for the next six to twelve weeks.

After about four to six weeks, breast-fed babies may stool daily or every few days. There is a very large range of normal in breast-fed babies—they may even stool once a week. In general, as long as stools are soft and the baby is comfortable, don't worry about the frequency. Most doctors do not get concerned if the baby hasn't had a stool until after ten days. Some will even say two weeks.

Wet diapers should be changed around six to ten times a day. Babies should be moving out as much as they are putting in. If you're concerned about milk transfer, your lactation consultant can do a weighted feed (weighing the baby on a sensitive scale before and after). Milk transfer is truly important when dealing with pree-mies. You will definitely want to weigh the diapers and the baby. This will tell you exactly how many ounces of milk are being trans-ferred per feed.

Another important gauge of whether Baby is getting enough milk is weight gain. You'll see your pediatrician a few times in the first week to ensure the baby is regaining birth weight. (Newborns are born with extra fluid, which is lost and regained within the first couple of weeks after birth. This fluid can average between five and eleven ounces.)

This is why I say write down everything when troubleshooting any situation with your baby. That way you can run through the list of everything you have tried when talking to the doctor.

BREAST-FEEDING TWINS

Breast-feeding twins is much more efficient than feeding one. It's as if you've opened a can of soda at both ends, and the liquid comes pouring out really fast. I like to see my moms feeding both babies at once. I teach them how to set themselves up in the middle of the bed, with the feeding pillow and both babies out in front. This way, if one of the babies rolls off your feeding pillow, there will be a safe soft spot for them to roll onto.

With twins, you're likely to have one strong and efficient sucker and one lazy one. (Just as you probably have one that sleeps like a dream and one that doesn't!) The efficient guzzler will work that breast and stimulate your milk production so that when you switch sides, the lazy eater will benefit from the increased flow from the breast they're now chomping on.

You should have each one feed for the first ten or fifteen minutes on one side and then switch, even if they're latched on well. They will need to burp, for one. But also, if one falls asleep, the last thing you want is to have Baby #1 feeding for forty-five minutes and Baby #2 waking up just as Baby #1 is ready to go down. If the twins are on different schedules and never sleep at the same time, you won't either!

So, what do you do when you have a sleepy twin? You already know! You down-dress to the diaper, wipe them down with a cool washcloth, or tickle their feet to keep them awake.

Some of my moms of twins feel like Jersey cows being herded into the barn and hooked up to the milking machines. When this happens, I sit with them and tell them this phase is going to pass before they know it, and they're doing a phenomenal job—times two.

Dealing with Knots in Your Breasts

Your milk has a long road to travel—from the back of your breast to the nipple—and it's common to get knots under your boobs on the far right and left sides. You don't have lumpy milk—you just have clogged ducts. These knots can be very painful, leaving your breasts tender and sore. This is why it is suggested that you do not wear underwire bras. They can make a tender and sore situation feel a hell of a lot worse. Remember: practical trumps beautiful!

If this happens, heat will be your BBF—Breast's Best Friend. A heating pad or heated washcloth can soften those ducts, which in turn helps the milk flow like the mighty Mississippi. In addition, taking a warm or hot shower around feeding times will assist your milk flow.

If heat doesn't work, here are a few more tactics:

+ Stimulate your breast by making circular motions on the sides of your breast and working your way to the nipple.

+ Sleep on your side or back. Remember: no sleeping on your stomach.

+ Since your baby and breast share a sixth sense, put your baby in the bed next to you or directly on your breast. Or let your partner get a few feels to get your girls started and then send them on their merry way so your baby can take over!

+ If all else fails, your pump is an effective artificial stimulant.

Mastitis Needs Immediate Treatment

Mastitis, an infection of the breast tissue and/or ducts, can strike with no warning. In my many years of dealing with breast-feeding moms, mastitis tends to show up when the milk ducts are not being completely emptied. It's nothing to play with, so contact your doctor *first*. There are also treatments you can do at home immediately, but they don't, of course, substitute speaking to your physician.

The symptoms of mastitis are a flu-like achy body, fever, and chills. They come on like a tidal wave—you simply get knocked out. You'll notice your breasts are hot and hard, and red streaks may even appear. You'll be feeling pretty crappy when it all starts, and within the next thirty minutes, you'll feel even worse. If you're very worried, reach out to your doctor, who can either call in a prescription or tell you the same thing I would—which is use a hot compress, get the baby back on your breast as soon as possible, and keep them informed of your progress.

There is nothing to fear, but you will want immediate relief. Don't make yourself suffer unnecessarily. Rest assured, most doctors recommend you keep on breast-feeding even with mastitis.

At-Home Mastitis Treatments

Your breasts will need a gentle circular massage to break up the milk. The best way to relieve mastitis is to get the baby to eat, even though the thought of a newborn getting near your unbearably hot and painful breasts makes you want to scream.

You can also use warm compresses or showers to unclog ducts. The heat from the washcloth or shower should provide you with instant relief. Making circular motions around the painful area with the heat also helps break up the milk in those ducts.

Emily Blunt: "Connie made me weep with laughter when mastitis hit. She would hold a warm compress to my boobs as she poured me a beer while declaring, 'Some people say take fenugreek—I say have a beer!'"

You should start to see results within a matter of hours. Once that milk starts flowing, you are going to want to ice down your breast to help slow those ducts until the baby can help you with sucking properly. I have noticed that some ducts become a little damaged after being clogged and produced less milk. This is common, so don't stress—there's really nothing you can do about it.

PUMP IT UP!

It's time to introduce your boobs to another new best friend—the breast pump. Warning: Your partner may get a little jealous because this pump will be getting more boob action than they'll ever see.

Breast pumps look very intimidating at first, but don't feel overwhelmed. The hoses, nozzles, bottles, and suction cups all have a purpose. You will become a pro very quickly as your breasts adjust to all the pumping.

After the first few days to a week, use your pump for a few quick minutes after feeding. This will send a message to your breasts to keep that production going. You are stimulating your breasts so when the baby comes back for the next feeding, there will be more for them to eat. Eventually, you won't have to do this prep work because your cups will start to runneth over. And over.

You should be using a pumping machine through your third week, when you can decrease to four times a day.

Pumping Chart

Keep a pumping journal just as you keep a breast-feeding journal. Make sure you jot down the breast your baby ate off last and how long they were on. This helps you keep your breasts in balance and your milk flow even. The more the baby eats, the more milk you will have.

Ashley McMahon and My Favorite Pumping Story

Ashley hails from Signal Mountain, Tennessee, and her husband, Joel, comes from a very prominent family in Birmingham, Alabama. She is my bubbly Southern belle and a diehard Alabama fan—so much that she named her second son Bryant after Bear Bryant. She's also a former clogger. (Yes, you read right, a clogger.) With Ashley, it was nothing but laughs and love.

"You know instantly that Connie is a baby whisperer. My firstborn, Thomas, was happiest slung over her shoulder with her patting his back. She nicknamed him 'Fruit Juicy,' which I called him way after it was appropriate. (Now when I am around people who coo and give babies funny nicknames, I know they are maternal people like Connie.)

"Connie had already taken care of my nephew three months prior, so I knew she was a hoot. She has the gift of being in your home, taking care of things, and socializing, but never feeling like a guest you must entertain, and immediately becoming part of the family. My husband has a teenage boy's sense of humor, but nothing he said ever rattled her. She'd just laugh and say, 'Boy, you crazy'—and if he tried anything when she was cooking, she'd swat him away with a spatula. I shudder to think about those first two weeks had I not had her in my life. She brought me joy, put my nerves at ease, and, most importantly, made me laugh.

"When I think back to Thomas's birth, I have such mixed emotions. It was not the birthing experience I had expected. I had to have an emergency C-section, and Thomas was swept up to the NICU while I remained in the hospital for a week undergoing tests, apart from my baby. As I laid in that hospital bed, no lactation consultant came by, so I read the books and told my husband a newborn is supposed to breast-feed every three hours for about twenty minutes. So, he woke me up every three hours, and I pumped into these little bottles. Then he would run them up to the NICU where Thomas was. By the end of the week, my husband had a bottle in between each finger, and the nurses were screaming, 'Make her stop! We have enough bottles in here to feed the entire nursery!'

"I went home a few days later with fully engorged size Gs. After a few days at home with Connie actually teaching me about the whole breast-feeding thing, I started running another fever. Connie ran out to buy frozen peas. I put them on to no avail, so she said we had to massage them down. 'I don't want you to think I am getting fresh, but you need some release,' she said as she started massaging my breasts with the frozen peas. I was practically moaning because it felt so good.

"Naturally, my husband chose just that moment to come into the nursery, and his eyes practically fell out of his head. Connie's reply was the best: 'I promise you it's not what you're thinking! I am getting her relief, and we don't want her back in the hospital.' We still laugh about it to this day."

What Ashley didn't add to this story was how painfully large and debilitating her breasts had become, they were a triple G. Every day, she'd be in tears, and we would sit for hours with ice. I would massage her breasts one at a time and put anti-inflammatory witch hazel on them to get things back on track. We were very worried that Thomas could be smothered, as we couldn't even see his head during a feeding. It took about a month and a half before Ashley's breasts slowly got back to normal, and it was a happy day for us both when she was no longer in so much pain.

Storing Your Breast Milk

In all my years of dealing with breast-feeding mothers, there has always been one constant question: "How long can fresh milk sit out before it goes bad?" If you live in a very cool house, your pumped milk can sit out for at least six hours. If your house is standard room temperature, fresh breast milk can sit out for up to four hours. If you like to keep your house warm, your milk needs to go in the refrigerator ASAP. Remember, heat is conducive to bacteria growth, and you don't want that!

Refrigerated breast milk can last for up to seventy-two hours. After seventy-two hours, you need to start freezing it. The first-out rule applies, so always use your oldest milk first. Frozen breast milk can last up to twelve months and should be frozen in quantities of two to three ounces.

Milk-storage bags are great, but Ziploc freezer bags are just as good. Label the bags by month, year, and time. Then place them flat in a square container (Tupperware, Rubbermaid) so the milk is dispersed in a thin layer. Once frozen, stack the individual packs in a gallon-size Ziploc bag and place back in the freezer to ensure a longer freezer life.

Defrosting Your Frozen Breast Milk

There are two ways to defrost frozen breast milk. One is to let it thaw at room temperature. This is your best bet since the bacterial growth starts much more slowly using this method. Milk thawed at room temperature is good for four hours and can stay in the refrigerator for twenty-four hours.

The second way is to use hot water. Milk dipped in the water like a tea bag will be ready instantly and is good for three hours in the refrigerator.

Never ever, ever, ever microwave breast milk! Even the most conscientious moms sometimes mess up and miss that thawing window, but stay away from the microwave. The heated milk can severely burn your baby.

Discard all breast milk that has been thawed and left out regardless of whether you used it. If it's been sitting out all day, do not feed this to your baby. You run the risk of three issues: bacteria building up in the milk, forgetting to put a clean nipple on that bottle—which puts the baby at high risk of getting thrush in their mouth—and the dissolution of the antibodies.

INTRODUCING BREAST MILK AND FORMULA

Jessica Biel: "She endured my fear of formula and even made a complicated homemade formula recipe for Silas to eat, which included fresh liver. We combined everything into the blender, but because it was boiling hot, the concoction exploded all over the kitchen and all over Nanny Connie. Sorry, Nanny!"

Introducing a bottle early on is so important. Whether it's a bottle full of expressed breast milk or formula, you want your baby to know that your nipple, as well as a rubber nipple, will give them the nourishment they need.

Why You Might Need to Use Both Breast Milk and Formula

1 Your baby might not like breast-feeding.

2 Your baby might need supplemental feeding, especially fat, and formula will give them that.

3 You might want to transition from breast-feeding to formula feeding.

If you're choosing to feed both breast milk and formula from a bottle, never mix them together. Feed the breast milk first, because if a baby does not take a full feeding you have wasted precious liquid gold. You can always purchase more formula, but you can't buy breast milk!

When to Introduce the Bottle

You should introduce the bottle by the third week. If you wait any longer, the baby will get used to eating from your breast exclusively, and it'll be harder to get them to eat from the bottle.

For the best latch, go nose to chin so they can smell the milk and root for it like little puppies. This will give you the same latch on the nipple of a bottle that you will get on your breast.

Many people believe that if you give a baby a bottle, they'll get nipple confusion, but that's not true. Babies just want their food! Preemies, after all, are bottle-fed in the NICU, and they come home and happily go right to the breast.

Normally, when my babies are drinking both, I give them breast milk during the day and formula at night. Let your partner start off with a formula feeding. This way you are able to see the reaction and also monitor the feeding. Most babies have no issue transitioning, as formula, especially an organic brand, is so similar to breast milk (which is still a little bit sweeter) that it rarely is refused.

Now that your partner will be helping feed the baby, take the training wheels off. You go to bed at ten o'clock and let your partner feed the baby—even though you secretly know they won't do it the way you want. This isn't about you, of course—it's about your partner and baby getting bonding time, as well as for your partner to feel confident and empowered without anyone looking over their shoulder. If they mess up, it's okay!

WHAT TO DO WHEN BREAST-FEEDING ISN'T WORKING

There are many little blessings who look at an areola as a bull's-eye and latch on like they were practicing in the womb. But then they decide, for whatever reason, that they've had it. They'll let you know through the universal newborn protest—three parts screaming plus one part body convulsions for dramatic flair!

When it's time to stop, just stop. It's perfectly normal. Just because your baby doesn't want your milk directly from your breast doesn't mean they will be deprived of breast milk—they can still enjoy it from a bottle. When you make the switch, you will see the angels, hear the celestial hymns, listen to the bluebirds chirping, and finally get some sleep.

For some babies, drinking from the breast is like Cinderella's stepsisters trying to shove their feet into her glass slipper. It's never going to happen! If a baby refuses the breast, guess who's in charge? It isn't you. Trust me when I say that some babies are just not breast-feeding babies and never will be. They don't latch on. They just slide off.

Of course, you're going to get stressed if this happens, but that will lower your milk production. The baby can sense that and will be even less inclined to latch on. But even if your baby won't breast-feed, you are not a failure.

You just had a baby. *Amazing!* Honestly, this is nothing more than a bump in the middle of the road.

FORMULA FEEDING

As you know by now, some babies just don't like the breast. And some moms, especially those who have to get back to work when the baby is only a few weeks old, find it very difficult to breast-feed and/or pump, so the best choice for them is formula.

Choosing the Best Formula for Your Baby

All formula sold in the United States is highly regulated and must contain all the nutrients a baby needs for growth and proper nutrition. The best formula for your baby is the one that they like, that causes as few digestive issues as possible, and that you can afford. You absolutely do not need to stick to any formula if you or your baby aren't happy with it! Bear in mind that no one—the hospital, your friends, even your pediatrician—will know the right formula better than your very own baby. (Just so you know, my favorite is Holle brand because you don't need a dictionary to read the ingredients. It meets all of the standards for your infant.)

Some formula, you will notice, can cause constipation. Sometimes it is not evident right away, but after awhile you may see the baby straining. If so, you should switch. There are many choices available: cow, soy, camel, organic, lactose-free, and goat.

Throughout my years of dealing with formulas, one question that has come up repeatedly is whether or not goat's milk is good for your baby. The answer is yes. Most people find when coming off breast-feeding, the protein base in goat milk is the most comparable to breast milk. In Europe it's a common practice for moms who are breast-feeding to use goat milk as supplemental milk. Check with your pediatrician about goat milk, though, as some believe it shouldn't be consumed until six months.

No one formula is better than another. I had a mom who decided the best formula was in Europe because their standards are slightly different than those of the Food and Drug Administration (FDA), but all the formula-fed babies I've taken care of have been just fine, whether they're drinking formula from Europe or from the United States.

Know Your Family Medical History

Your baby's genetic makeup is a huge factor. If you are lactose intolerant, your child stands a chance of inheriting this, and you may see your baby having trouble feeding or becoming constipated. It can sometimes take up to a month for you to notice any issues.

What If You Don't Have Access to Your or Your Baby's Medical History?

If you used IVF technology or a sperm/egg donor, try to get as detailed a medical history as possible from the donors, as this will help not just with formula but also with all future medical issues.

If you don't have this information or if your baby is adopted and no information is provided, you will have to be cautious when trying different formulas until you find one your baby tolerates well.

Add an Ounce of Water

Years ago, when I was a baby, my mom would feed me formula, followed by a little bit of sterile water. Adding an extra ounce of water to a formula bottle can make all the difference in the world. Formula-fed babies seem to strain more when trying to poop as the formula moves through their digestive systems. That extra ounce of water makes things flow much easier. Some pediatricians don't think the baby's kidneys are mature enough for a straight bottle of water; that's why I add just an extra ounce of water in the bottle. However, I suggest you speak to your doctor before you add additional water to formula.

Switching Formula

Keep the baby on the formula you're using for at least one week before deciding it's not a good choice. If you need to switch, go cold turkey—no mixing. If you do, you won't know which formula might be causing the issues. Hand off any extra formula to another mother who can use it.

Powdered vs. Liquid Formula

There is no difference between liquid and powder formulas, except liquid formulas are way more expensive. I like powder because you have more control over that extra ounce of water, and it's more portable. Once opened, liquid must be used or refrigerated, so for all your extra helpers who may not know better, powder is key.

Organic vs. Regular Formula

I recommend organic formula. Organic ingredients seem to be more easily tolerated by most babies' digestive tracts. It's more expensive, but you want your formula to be as pure as possible. It shouldn't contain any additives, coloring, or chemicals that aren't totally necessary.

Should Formula Be Warmed Up?

Nope! When breast milk comes out of your body, it is actually a little chilled, so room temperature is perfect for formula. You don't want to be out somewhere and have to warm water to make your bottle because that's the only way your baby will drink it.

There Is *No Shame* in Bottle Feeding!

No mom should ever feel shamed for bottle feeding. You simply cannot make a baby take a breast if that baby does not want to breast-feed. You are not a failure. Your baby can still get that liquid gold out of a bottle.

It's amazing, isn't it, how our attitude toward breast-feeding has shifted over the last few decades? In the 1950s and 1960s, it was basically taboo to breast-feed. Women just didn't do it. Or, if they did, they went into a quiet room and locked the door, and no one was allowed anywhere near them. It was almost like the mom had a disease or was snickered at because she couldn't afford formula. Ridiculous, right?

INTRODUCING SOLIDS

At four months, bottle- and breast-fed babies now have something in common. You can start to incorporate solid food into their diet, such as oatmeal, avocado, mashed-up roasted butternut squash, and stewed apples or pears. I know how hard it is to find the time to cook, especially if you've gone back to work, so my best tip is to peel and cut up chunks of lots of different veggies and roast them until they're soft. Then you can put them through a food mill or a blender, freeze them (use a silicon ice cube tray!), and have meals for a couple of weeks. All healthy and unprocessed homemade food is so much cheaper—and more delicious—than buying baby food.

When you start to introduce solids, do not add salt or sugar to any of the food. (Butter, on the other hand, is a different story. Butter makes everything better.) What's bland to you is delicious and flavorful to a baby who's tasting it for the first time.

I learned this thanks to my very difficult pregnancy with Courtney. My doctors finally realized our blood types were incompatible, so by my fourth month, I was in the hospital at least twice a month for one complication or another. One of the restrictions I had was no salt. I mean, not even a grain. Luckily, my mom was there to cook for me, and she made amazing, simple meals.

Fast-forward to after Courtney was born and I was able to eat without restrictions. It tasted like my mom had over-seasoned the food because my taste buds were so salt free. It was a good lesson for me not to salt food for my babies, who also aren't used to the taste.

FILL 'ER UP! ALL BABIES HAVE GAS

It doesn't matter how you feed your baby—all babies are still going to have gas.

I was in the grocery store once and saw a lovely, very well-put-together young mom pushing her son in a top-of-the-line stroller. I could hear him crying as I rounded the meat department, and as I headed for the checkout, I could hear his cry change gears as if I were downshifting in a brand-new Porsche. I told the cashier to please put my groceries to the side and went back to ask if she needed assistance. She said she was looking for formula, and my heart sank. I gently asked why she hadn't removed her baby from the stroller. She answered me with the same puzzled expression all moms have and said, "He's just going to have to go right back in when he gets to the car." I asked if I could pick him up, and when I unlocked her baby from his stroller, his face seemed to say, "Thank you, Jesus, for sending me an angel." I pulled his legs straight, and the loudest burp came from the little fellow. He looked as if he had just won the lottery. The mom was completely stunned.

I explained to her that a little baby is just learning how to swallow properly, and any time he cries as he swallows, he will have a stomach full of gas. I recommended gas drops to help with the situation.

She was so grateful. "No one's ever told me any of this," she said as she gave me a hug, and I wished her well. Everyone had been judging her and giving her the stink-eye because her baby wouldn't stop crying. They thought she wasn't being attentive—but she just didn't know what to do.

Why Babies Have Gas

+ A baby is learning how to swallow. They aren't yet used to having a large amount of anything in their mouths. So naturally they swallow air.

+ With growth comes room, and with room comes air. When a baby's stomach starts to expand as they grow, it takes awhile for the baby to adjust. They tend not to eat to full capacity initially. (This happens frequently during growth spurts.) That extra room is full of air, which produces gas.

+ Every time babies cry, they swallow air. The longer or more aggressively they cry, the more air they swallow, producing more gas.

+ If you are a breast-feeding mother and you've eaten something very gassy (like veggies) or highly spiced, your baby will be gassy, too.

+ An improper bottle angle will cause the baby to gulp air while feeding. Angle the baby on a nice slant; you don't want them being flat. This helps to reduce the gulps of air.

+ Feeding your baby and then placing them directly in their car seat is a recipe for gas disaster, as the gas will be trapped in a restrained baby, unable to be expelled, leading to discomfort and crying.

Babies Need Gas Drops

Gas is really painful for babies, and that, as you know, leads to distress—a.k.a. screaming at the top of their lungs, which only produces more gas. Some babies also have more serious reflux that can't be dealt with by regular burpings and can morph from simple gas pain to chronic stomach problems.

That's why gas drops are a must. They help neutralize the gastric acids in your baby's stomach.

How to Choose and Use Gas Drops

Gas drops are all pretty much the same. I don't really have a preference, though I prefer gas drops over gripe water because they provide a faster result.

The problem is that most parents use gas drops very sparingly, which is wrong. Don't exceed the dosage on the box, but remember they should be used aggressively in the beginning because there are many reasons for gas that we don't even think of, like those gulps you hear when they're feeding. Your baby is likely to spit out most of the gas drops anyway, so it's hard at first to even get the minimal amount in their bodies!

My solution is to give a baby a dosage of gas drops before each feeding. This helps to break up the gas before they eat.

Don't be afraid of gas drops. There is no way they can harm your baby, and they are guaranteed to diminish your baby's gas problem. Always have them handy and keep them near where you feed at home and in your diaper bag.

How to Burp Your Baby

I love teaching new parents about burping. They're so sweet and nervous about holding their precious little bundle and so worried about dropping the baby. Most will give a gentle tap, say, "Okay, all done," but this is where I say, "Hell, naw, dawg, there is more to come!" We are in search of that all-mighty beer burp. The baby's not going to break—pat a little harder! A good burp is a very loud burp. Don't be shocked at how much gas can come out of such a tiny body.

I worked with one dad whose son was a champion burper with me. I told him he'd know when it happens, but he looked skeptical. I walked him through the whole process and the baby let rip a really good one. In fact, it sounded just like his dad after his evening beer. Dad looked so panic-stricken that I couldn't help but laugh.

"Now that," I said to him, "is the sound you're looking for. So, tell me why you look so startled."

"Because," Dad said, "did you hear that shit? I thought that was you!"

The best way to burp the baby is to hold their legs long and their arms across your shoulder, and then straighten out those legs and anchor them with one hand to give their diaphragms the stretch they need to push out the gas.

As long as babies keep pulling those legs up, gas will be moving. As soon as they relax those legs, you've conquered gas and have a happy baby with a nice full belly who's going to fall asleep without any fuss.

Dealing with Spit-up

Yes, all babies do spit up, usually when you've just put on a nice clean blouse!

It doesn't matter if you're breast-feeding or bottle feeding—spit-up is going to happen. Now, sometimes if the breast-feeding mother has cracked nipples there will be specks of blood in the spit-up. This is quite common and perfectly okay! And to answer the question rolling around in your mind right now . . . hell yes, that's going to hurt and sting like a [insert your own adjective]. But that's a part of life!

Spit-up happens when your baby's digestive system isn't fully developed and because babies always swallow air when they're feeding. When this air comes out in the form of a burp, it's easy for a bit of breast milk or formula to come up with it. This is totally normal, which is why I suggested you get at least one or two dozen cloth diapers to use as burp cloths.

Some babies are projectile vomiters; it's true that even a very tiny baby can spit up across the room. You should completely cover your feeding chairs and yourself during feeding times and expect that there will be more milk on you than in the baby. If this happens consistently, you should reach out to your pediatrician because you might need to either switch formula or give the baby prescribed medicine. Pay close attention if your baby doesn't want to eat, starts wheezing, or cries constantly for no reason. Take any baby with persistent vomiting to your pediatrician right away.

Let's Talk About Colic

Colic terrifies most parents, even though few know what causes it. I can't tell you how many of my parents thought their babies had colic but had no idea what colic was. Colic is endless hours with an inconsolable baby, strapping the baby in the car seat and driving aimlessly for hours in an attempt to soothe them, or putting the baby on the washing machine so the rhythmic motion lulls them out of their crying and into sleep.

Colic can seem like someone has taken over your child's body at the same time every day! I deal with it as if it were an intruder. So when I see it coming, I know what to do. Knock on wood! I have never had a baby suffer from colic because I use gas drops from day one. I honestly don't understand why pediatricians don't tell new parents to use them. If you feed your baby the right way, chances are very slim that colic will rear its ugly head.

Babies are often misdiagnosed with colic way too soon. It doesn't just show up out of the blue. It evolves. Try taming the situation with regular use of gas drops and my burping method before you go to the doctor. Obviously if the situation persists or gets worse, seek medical advice, but hopefully your new BFF will nip this situation in the bud before it has a chance to become an issue.

chapter seven

PEE, POOP, AND BABY-SCAPING

John Krasinski: John always stood right by my side soaking everything in. He watched me with the bath from start to finish. He actually filmed me to be sure that he didn't miss a beat. It took him two attempts at bath time before he was moving like a ninja. By the time Miss Violet came along, the roles reversed, and I was filming John! I'd smile when I saw him achieve something he learned. He had this look of success that shined across his entire face. It was great to see all the things John had learned from Hazel and to see how confident and relaxed he was when it came to Violet.

DIAPER DAZE

Babies are truly amazing peeing and pooping machines. Their digestive systems are still new and underdeveloped, so whatever goes in is going to quickly come out the other end. This is why so many parents who swore they were going to use cloth diapers suddenly change their minds!

How Many Diapers Will You Need?

Expect to change between seven and ten diapers each day, or up to seventy diapers a week.

Newborns grow incredibly quickly, and few stay in the newborn size for more than two or three weeks, if that. My rule of thumb is when the tabs move from meeting in the middle right under the baby's navel to almost reaching their sides, your diaper is too snug, and it's safe to move your baby to the next size.

Once you jump into a size, expect to stay there for up to six weeks. Buy in bulk, so you don't have to worry about running out, and keep at least two cases in the closet to supply your diaper bag and have at least a few weeks' worth of backup.

What You're Going to See in the Diapers

Pee Time

Your little one is likely to be peeing more than you think. Diapers are so advanced now that they come with indicators that change color when peed in.

Every wet diaper doesn't need to be changed immediately. Babies pee all day long, and each time it's about 20 ccs, or 1.3 tablespoons. Disposable diapers are super-absorbent, so you don't have to pull a pee-only diaper off right away because infants can pee up to four to six times before the diaper is saturated. Check the weight or the color indicator on the baby's diaper so you know when it's getting full.

Poop Time for Breast-fed Babies

Don't be surprised by the texture, color, or frequency of a breast-fed newborn's poop diaper. The color and texture will resemble mustard seed and cottage cheese, and most sound like a loud explosion. Although this explosion can happen up to three times in a feeding, there will be little to nothing in the diaper when you go to change it.

Breast-fed babies' stool has very little or no odor at all, until a few months later when their intestines are better able to process food.

It's imperative that you start each feeding with a clean diaper so you don't have to take your baby off the breast for a changing.

Around months 2 and 3, you can expect an explosion every diaper change. You won't have to guess if the diaper is wet or if there's a present for you inside. You'll know!

Poop Time for Formula-fed Babies

I can always look at a diaper and know if it's from breast milk or formula. Formula poop has a mixture of color due to the fact that formula has more additives than breast milk, and its consistency is more like Play-Doh. A formula-fed baby's poop also has a unique aroma!

They will also average fewer poops a day than a breast-fed baby.

In months 2 and 3, stool will have a little more color (darker and maybe some yellow) and a lot more smell.

Poop Time for Solid Foods

Now you have moved into the aromatherapy diapers. As soon as your baby starts eating solids, their stool will change color and texture (becoming more solid and pastier), and smell even worse. You have been warned! That delicately wafting aroma will make you glad you are such a pro at changing diapers in a hurry.

How to Change a Diaper

When it comes to putting diapers on baby boys, make sure to always point their penis downward before securing the diaper. This gives your newborn a nice little cubby area to catch the pee and stop it from wetting their clothes in the middle of the night. This works time and time again, especially with explosive diapers, as the poop doesn't just shoot out the diaper, but rather, into the pocket.

With all babies, you must pay very close attention to those indicators that let you know when the diapers are full. This is the first line of defense for avoiding diaper rash. Always try to contour diapers around the baby's waist for a nice snug fit to keep their clothes from getting wet. Always fold your diaper in, not out, to make for a neater diaper. Be sure to fold the decorative band area halfway down to help keep all the wetness and poop inside the diaper.

How to Wipe Properly

There is no need to wipe and wipe and wipe! Think of the opening up of the diaper as your first wipe. Open it, pull down the front, wipe down, and tuck it. Then come in with your wipes.

Even with a diaper full of poop, you will rarely need more than three wipes. Wiping for a wet-only diaper is more like blotting, because the urine is not as strong or potent as an adult's.

With girls, you always want to wipe front to back, never pulling the lips of their privates open to dig anything out. If it is a very messy situation, you'll want to put her bottom under warm running water instead of irritating her private area by digging.

With boys, you want to lift the testicles and wipe side to side. For a non-circumcised baby, pull back the head of the penis to make sure no poop has gotten stuck under the foreskin. Don't worry if some of the poop ends up on your hand. It happens to the best of us. Welcome to parenthood!

How to Use Diaper Cream

A tube of my favorite Boudreaux's Butt Paste has lasted me an entire year. That's how little diaper cream you need! No need to slather it on unless your baby has a severe case of diaper rash and your pediatrician tells you to. Diaper cream is not caulk; it's just a protective barrier for the outside of those chubby little butt cheeks. Simply squeeze the butt (and, for girls, the lips of the vagina) together and apply a thin layer of cream. If you apply it to the folds, the buildup will be a job in itself to remove.

Diaper Disposal

You don't want to discard an open diaper, but instead convert it into a neat little ball by rolling it up and using the tabs on the diaper to tape it shut to avoid mess and stink. You can also buy deodorized disposal bags, which are handy when you are out in public.

How to Change Without a Changing Table

One of the staples in your diaper bag should be a portable changing pad. My favorite is a rubber pad, because it becomes very soft over time, making it easy to pack. Make sure yours is lightweight, easy to clean, and waterproof. Never change a diaper on any surface without a changing pad and always have everything you need out before opening the diaper. Never leave a baby on a surface unattended because you have forgotten something you need.

How to Change on a Public Changing Table or at a Friend's House

Make sure you put down your baby's changing pad on top of the changing table and repeat the same steps mentioned above. Always wash your hands and the baby's hands thoroughly with warm soapy water when in a public restroom. If soap is not available, use hand sanitizer.

It's simple. It's all about confidence and experience. Keep your eyes on the prize. The more you look around and worry someone is going to see something or say something, the longer it'll take to finish the job. You can do it!

Changing a Baby on a Plane

A small confined space surrounded by strangers with nowhere to go sounds like the perfect situation to change a diaper. Don't break out in a cold sweat—you've got this. These quick steps will make you look like a pro even if it's a blowout diaper.

+ Do everything in your power to time your flight to take off just before the baby's nap, so you will have less changing to worry about. No parent wants to do a change on a plane, but for long or delayed flights, you're going to have to suck it up and get it done.

+ I like to have the inside window seat rather than the aisle because you can contain your movements more easily, and if you have to change a diaper, you can simply put the baby on your lap. Use a cover, such as a lightweight blanket, if you are worried about the people in your row saying something. The odor of a baby's diaper is not going to be that potent or linger for any length of time, so focus on the task, and it'll be done more quickly than the time it would take for you to get up and walk down the aisle to the bathroom.

✦ An airplane bathroom is barely large enough for an adult. Do not take your baby in there for a change. It's very difficult to maneuver, much less find the surface area you need to do the deed. Even if the ride is perfectly smooth when you get up, there is always the possibility of unexpected turbulence, which can seriously harm both you and your baby.

✦ Practicing at home will make for a perfect plane ride and help you become an expert in placing the dirty diaper in your deodorized bag before anyone notices. Remember: chess, not checkers. Practice makes perfect.

✦ For a long-haul flight, request a bassinet to use in the bulkhead seats. It's very easy to do the changes when your baby is in the bassinet because no one will even know.

BABY-SCAPING: CARE FOR BABIES' BODIES

When I was working with a mother of twins in Fairhope, Alabama, she would peer into the room as if her kids were aliens. I finally asked her what she was afraid of. I thought to myself: was she scared of catching me in my underwear or coming out of the shower? But, really, she was just terrified of what she called the limp-and-drool stage.

Like this mom, so many parents are really afraid of babies, as if they're fragile porcelain. One of the things that scares them the most is that they're afraid of a tiny, floppy little creature that seems boneless. But babies are a lot tougher than they look. Every parent experiences the nightmare of rolling over onto their child or dropping them, but trust that it's not going to happen on your watch. You don't want the baby to pick up on how tense you are. Relax! You're the parent. The baby knows you by scent and sound and is already automatically soothed by your very presence.

How to Hold Your Baby

Cradling the head and supporting the back is crucial. When you pick up a baby, one hand should go under the upper quadrant—the shoulder blades to the nape of the neck—and one hand should go to the base of their head. Always put a burp cloth between you and the baby.

Because your hands are so large in proportion to the baby, you will practically be holding their entire body in this kind of hold. As long as you're supporting that neck and it's not wobbling around like the lotto balls in the back barrel, you're good!

One of the reasons this proper hold is so important is that when your baby is tired, they have absolutely no muscle tone and get even floppier than usual. Holding your baby so securely also gives you the direct eye contact for the conversations you're going to be having that are so important for your bonding. This is a better position than merely cradling, as they can start sliding down in your arms, and you can't really see them that well.

If you're worried about holding your baby while breast-feeding, arrange your feeding station to be on a wide surface so you can move around and be comfortable and, if for some reason the baby slips, they'll fall on something soft and no damage will be done. I always tell parents to practice elbow to hand on the bed: put your elbow on the bed and then cradle the baby with the palm of your hand on their back and hold with the other hand.

Nothing makes me feel better than seeing a dad walking around and giving his buddies advice and tips on how to hold their babies. They go from being terrified about picking up something so small to doing the tucking-in and then, when the baby is a bit older, the football carry, walking around like they've just scored a touchdown. I never tell a dad he's doing a hold or a carry wrong. I just ask him if he wants to see a demonstration, and when he knows he's got it down, he visibly blossoms with confidence.

Baby Grooming

Umbilical Cord Care

Why are you trying to pickle it? Leave it alone, and it will be just fine. Don't try to pick the umbilical cord stump off; it's not the kind of scab you want to remove. All you have to do is use a cotton swab or ball dipped in a bit of rubbing alcohol once or twice a day and gently dab it on. This does not hurt the baby at all. If the scab starts to form together, it's about to come off, which usually happens within the first ten days to two weeks. It may bleed a little bit, but don't panic—this is normal.

Avoid putting a diaper on your baby for as long as possible on the night that the last bit falls off. You want to allow the navel to make that last little turn before totally folding in to become that sweet little belly button you're going to love to blow on when you're tickling your baby a few months from now.

Do not bathe your baby until the cord has completely fallen off and the belly button has closed up.

Circumcision Care

You should wait for the circumcision to heal before you start any daily hygiene. I have found that using Neosporin helps the area heal quicker.

With uncircumcised babies, keeping the penis clean is a must. You want to make sure you push the foreskin back and keep the ridge of the penis clean because a buildup can be very painful. For this reason, never use any lotions or creams on the penis.

Nail Trimming

Do not start trimming nails with baby nail clippers until babies are three months old. Filing with a glass emery board is always safer. An infant can't tell you that you are cutting too close, so you need to wait for the length of the nail to clear the base of the finger. I've seen so many parents collapse in tears when they tried to cut their babies' nails and drew blood instead. These nails can look really long, but they are still so tiny that it's very hard to get underneath them for a good trim.

Hair Brushing and Fontanels

If your baby has hair, gentle brushing with a soft brush is totally fine. Brushing stimulates the skin on the top of their head and reduces cradle cap. Combing a baby's head is not necessary.

Babies have two soft spots on their heads, on the front and the back, called fontanels. They're there for two reasons: to allow your baby's skull to be flexible during the birth, especially as your baby moves through the birth canal, and to allow your baby's brain and skull to grow during those early months. The back fontanel usually closes by two to four months, while the front one usually closes before the age of two.

I don't worry about hair brushing as much as I worry about people and their oily, germ-infested fingers touching the fontanels, which are more delicate than a fully fused skull. Make sure everyone washes their hands before handling the baby!

Oral Care

Keep pacifiers and bottle nipples clean and sterilized. There is no care needed for the baby's gums until the teeth start coming in, which is months away. You might want to buy one of those cute little rubber brushes you put on your finger now just to have it ready. Babies love them when they're starting to teethe. Just be aware that a baby's bite can be stronger than you think!

THE BATH-TIME RITUAL

I love bath time with Baby and trust that Baby loves it just as much. After over thirty years and countless baths, I've seen how wonderfully soothing and soporific it is for babies when their bath sets the mood for the end of the day. Same for you, of course—at the end of a long and tiring day, what could be more relaxing than a long soak in a hot tub, with soft music playing and a candle or two for atmosphere? It's the ideal way to get your body and soul ready for bed.

Before the Bath Starts

Prep work will make your bath time a breeze. While the water is running, get out your towel, pajamas, a clean diaper, any lotion you're using, a soft washcloth, and a brush if your baby has hair. Once the bath starts, you can never leave your baby unattended in the tub. Babies and small children can drown in a mere inch or two of water.

Use a Bath Sling or Hammock

A bathtub is way too big, slippery, and dangerous for an infant to ever be put in. You can use your kitchen sink or get a small baby-size tub instead, one that fits across the sink or comfortably on the counter in your kitchen or bath. Make sure the tub also offers a hammock.

This baby-bath hammock is phenomenal—one of the best inventions for babies I've ever seen. It supports the baby completely in the water and keeps their head securely elevated so parents (especially dads!) who might have been a bit nervous about managing a wet baby feel safe and secure during bath time. The sling allows you to be hands-free so you can move the baby's head and body any way you like to get to all the crevices.

When using a hammock tub, fill the water to just below the mesh of the hammock. Push the hammock down so it gets warmed up to the same temperature as the water. Then when you lay the baby down, they won't be startled by any disparity in the temperature.

Never submerge a baby's entire body at once. Put in their feet first, then their butt so they're in a sitting position. Lean the baby forward on your forearm, creating a cradling position. Using your other hand, put water on their back so they get used to it and then slowly lay them in the hammock. Once the baby feels supported, they instantly relax and calm down. Sometimes, though, their initial reaction is to pick their feet up, so move their legs gently up and down to give them the chance to adjust. They'll just lie there, blissful, like little puppies all stretched out and contented.

The Bathwater Needs to Be Very Warm

Remember your water breaking and the warm feeling rushing down your leg? Your baby does, too. A baby has spent nine months in your amniotic fluid the same temperature as your body, so why would they want to move from that nice warm uterus into a tepid bath? The water temperature should be hot enough so that by the end of the bath, it is still lukewarm. You don't want to see purple baby lips because the water has gotten cold!

If you are worried about the temperature, use a bath thermometer at first. After awhile, you'll know by touch alone.

How to Wash Your Baby

Make your baby's bath time a routine, and it'll be even more relaxing. Get into the habit of bathing your baby in front of the mirror; as they get older they will turn and look at themselves and be utterly transfixed! Use this time to talk to your baby. They will quickly associate the sound of your calm and happy voice with soothing and love, which will help get them ready for bed.

+ For the first month or two, all you need to clean your baby, especially their face, is water. (You really don't want to get soap into their eyes!) Breast milk is odorless, so the only thing that can leave a lingering scent is formula, or poop from a formula-fed baby—which, of course, you will have already wiped away. You just want to get into all those delicious little crevices and wipe them down. If you need to, use warm water and soap on their bottom half to remove any residual leftovers from the last diaper change.

+ Get into the habit of using a soft washcloth to ensure you reach every crevice. It will also teach your baby, once they get older, that a washcloth = good hygiene.

+ Wash the baby's face first. Start with the tear ducts. Place a soft wet washcloth between your thumb and index finger. Gently massage the ducts and pull out anything that's in there. You don't want to pick at it, but if something is not removed, it can clog up the tear ducts. When that happens, it's often mistaken for pink eye, which is highly contagious. Babies don't produce tears to flush out their ducts until they are three to four months old.

✦ The most important parts of your baby's body that you want to be as clean as possible are their hands and their butt. So many people will be reaching out to touch your baby, and if they are in onesies or pajamas, the only parts that are visible are their head and hands. And what do babies do with their hands after you've put your own paws on them? They put them in their mouths! Butts, for obvious reasons, need a quick check in case you missed anything.

✦ If you insist on using soap, it should be as pure, gentle, and organic as possible, as well as unscented. You can try Cetaphil bar soap or Aveeno liquid soap. Soap up a super-soft washcloth really well so you can clean the baby's body in one sweep without re-sudsing. Let the water out of the tub, leaving the baby in the hammock, and rinse. Fill a pitcher with warm water for a final rinse.

✦ If your baby has hair, cradle the head in the palm of your hand, put a tiny dab of organic, unscented shampoo on your baby brush, and rub gently in circular motions. Don't be afraid of the fontanel (the soft spot)—you won't hurt it. Rinse carefully to keep the water and suds away from the baby's face.

✦ Now if your baby boy is not circumcised, you are going to have to gently roll back the foreskin to make sure there's nothing in there. It's common for boys to have a bit of lint or buildup from cream or lotion in there. Simply wipe it away with warm water, not soap. (If you don't do this regularly, you might need to have the pediatrician check to see if there's any buildup.) Be gentle, as it can be extremely painful for a baby to have his foreskin manipulated.

✦ Baby girls' vaginas (or pocketbooks, as I like to say!) often have a little cottage-cheese-looking discharge—sometimes it even looks like dried glue—which is perfectly normal. Don't pick at or scrub it; just let it discharge itself. Simply pull back the lips of the pocketbook and wipe down what has discharged.

✦ When the baby is all clean, have your towel handy to swaddle them. Then take them to the changing table or bed, lay them down on a rubber pad or another soft towel, and pat them dry. The skin should be pink and bright—this is the heat of their body. When the skin is still slightly damp, massage for a few minutes with shea butter or moisturizing cream, which are always more effective when skin isn't totally dry (a good tip for you, too!)

chapter eight

THE TRIED-AND-TRUE SLEEP RITUAL

Matt and Lucy Damon: I can remember very vividly the stories Matt and Lucy told me of the tag-team bedtime process they went through for Isabella, before I came along. They told me how the room would be pitch black, how they would play a song over and over and over again, and how they had worn a path from walking back and forth with their new bundle. That was all they knew how to do.

Then the first of August came, and Little Miss Gia, their second bundle of joy, showed up. That's when my Sleep Ritual started. I set the mood with a warm bath, dimmed lights, soft music, and an after-bath massage. Once Gia was in her jammies, Matt and Lucy would come in, and Matt would feed her a nice bottle of breast milk. Then I placed Gia into her bassinet and just like that, she was off having a party with the Sandman.

Matt and Lucy looked at me like I was Houdini. They were amazed at how simple the process was. It became so enjoyable that my room became our hangout spot. From dessert to politics, the three of us would hang out in the room with all the children asleep until the next feeding time came at 11:00 p.m. or 12:00 a.m. Those were the days!

Sleep deprivation is real—no one is safe! Before you know it, you'll be in a heap of blubber on the floor, unable to function and beating yourself up for not being up to the tasks that seem to loom larger and more difficult with each passing night. You won't realize it until it smacks you in the face: After pulling an all-nighter to feed your angel, you'll be waiting for the coffeemaker to start before realizing you never hit the button. Then you'll want to pull a WWE move on your partner for getting the wrong kind of creamer, and before you know it, Niagara Falls is coming out of your tear ducts.

This is why I developed my Sleep Ritual for All Babies and All Parents, which will teach you how to sleep when the baby does. I start it on day one to calm your baby and make them feel safe, as well as soothe you and give you the confidence to rock that nighttime routine.

You already know, of course, that little kids pick up on how to ride a bike or roller skate pretty quickly. Learning how to do these as an adult takes much longer and is a lot scarier. Ditto with sleep training, so start it as soon as you can. Babies only know what you teach them! If you don't show them from day one, you can find yourself with a screaming, sleepless baby a few months later.

Have faith. The Sleep Ritual hasn't failed me yet.

Your baby is smart, and your baby likes routine. The Sleep Ritual will become so ingrained in your baby that by the time they're toddlers, they'll know that after dinner, they're going to go upstairs like sweet little soldiers, take a nice hot bath, turn the lights down, read a book, and hit the hay. Toddlers who have this routine down to a T look forward to it—the wonderful feeling of the warm bath, the smell of the diaper cream, your touch when putting on their jammies, the ultimate satisfaction of grabbing the pacifier and getting to suckle it all night long. Your friends are going to beg you to tell them how you did it, and I give you permission to spill the beans when you explain how brilliantly simple the Sleep Ritual is.

THE NIGHTTIME SLEEP RITUAL FOR YOUR BABY

Consistency is key! This is a baby sleepy-time assembly line. You're training your baby to expect that each step leads to the next one, and eventually to slumber.

1 Let the Baby Watch the Mobile While You Get the Bath Prepped
Set the temperature in the baby's room to 75 degrees Fahrenheit and place your baby near the mobile to keep them busy. Next, prep the bath and get everything you'll need laid out so you won't be fumbling for anything.

2 Warm Bath
You already know how important it is to have a warm bath. You never want the water to get chilly before bath time ends—it'll wake the baby up!

3 Lights Down
Turn your lights down low as a signal that it's time for bed. Put the humidifier on, adding a few drops of lavender or eucalyptus oil if you like, for relaxation, and lay out the baby's jammies.

4 Music

From the time you realized you were pregnant until the time your baby came into this world, you've been told to talk and talk so they can get used to the sound of your voice. Playing music for your baby is just as essential. So put on the music after you turn out the lights—or before the bath so it's already playing when you come out—and set the timer so the music will shut itself off by 12:30 or 1:00 a.m.

In Baby Land, their minds are going a thousand miles a second, and those melodies, rhythms, and beats help them relax. Once they hear familiar songs, they'll start falling asleep.

Choose music you love without vocals, which can wake your baby's brain up inadvertently. Ideally, you should play the same instrumental music you played when you were pregnant—your baby is clever enough to recognize it. Classical music and smooth jazz have a phenomenal influence on newborns and are beneficial to the growth and expansion of their little brains. George Winston, John Flucker, Mozart—take your pick. Shelve AC/DC and Lil Jon for now; they can have their day later.

I start my playlist from the day I start taking care of my babies, and all of my little ones have thoroughly enjoyed it. Take your time putting yours together. It's a really fun and challenging task, and you can mix up classical music like Mozart and Bach with contemporary jazz or New Age tunes. Teaching your baby to appreciate music is a gift. Not just because yours is going to grow up to be a prodigy, but music makes you think better, listen better, appreciate creativity more, and be better able to self-soothe.

Hearing the playlist will become a signal that bedtime is approaching. It might not seem that significant now, when your baby is so little and sleeping so much, but trust me—it is! You're establishing an excellent habit that will soothe your baby as they get older and the whining about bedtime starts. Ask my parents of toddlers!

As your baby gets older, turn off the music sooner. Instead of 1:00 a.m., have the timer go off by 11:00 p.m. This will help your baby get used to any ambient nighttime noise.

NOISE IS NOT THE ENEMY!

Don't make your baby's bedroom too quiet. Babies have heard voices and sounds for nine months. As a member of the family, your baby will soon realize that people talk to each other and make noise, so don't create an environment where you can hear a pin drop every time it's time to feed or rest.

A baby who can sleep with noise in the background can sleep anywhere. One day, one of my mothers left me a long voicemail, saying she'd gone out of town with her baby and four other moms with very small children. When bedtime arrived, all of her girlfriends were covering the windows in the room and turning up the white-noise machines, while her daughter had already been asleep for forty-five minutes. While the other moms were still fussing, she was sitting out on the beach watching the sunset and enjoying her second martini.

Addicting your child to a white noise machine is comparable to letting them sleep in a perfectly quiet room. If you decide to use one, it will become something you must do all the time. If you still want to use one, put it outside their bedroom door so it filters the noise coming into the room, and continue to play their soothing music at bedtime.

5 Massage Time

After the bath, put your baby on the changing table or in the middle of the bed. Put a little bit of organic, unscented shea butter in the palm of your hand to warm it up. Then start massaging it into your baby's skin, using small, gentle strokes. Begin with those delectable dumpling butt cheeks, move up their back and down their legs, then flip the baby over and do their chest, belly area, and arms. Avoid their hands, though, as they will put their fingers in their mouths. Since the baby will still be warm from the bath, the shea butter will absorb very quickly into their skin and it won't get pasty or sticky (another reason why I like it).

6 Jammies
When you're done with the massage, wipe off any excess shea butter, then dress the baby with a clean diaper, undershirt, socks, and jammies.

ABOUT THOSE JAMMIES

by Amy Spottswood, a mom from that initial
circle in Mobile, Alabama, in which I was passed
around like a hot biscuit out of the oven

One evening Nanny Connie dressed our daughter Macy for bed, giving me an opportunity to take a much-needed bath. Feeling relaxed, I settled in to nurse Macy and noticed her pajamas were on backward. Being a first-time mom and thinking everything had to be perfect, I glanced up to Nanny Connie to mention the faux pas. Before I even said a word, she just giggled, looked at my three-day-old, and said, "I told ya she'd notice!" We burst out laughing, and, I must admit, I switched the pajamas around. Nanny Connie always lightened up stressful situations with her confidence and humor.

Nanny Connie was a ray of warm, loving sunshine to our family during very happy but hectic and scary times. Her sunshine was radiant, her wise counsel unsurpassed, and her nurturing nature heaven-sent. Her laughter was warmer than a bright Christmas fire, her smile drove peaceful pleasantness deep into my soul, and her countenance reflected the joy a family should experience with the birth of a young life. She was *way better* than Mary Poppins!

7 Optional: Reading Time
If your baby seems wide awake after the massage and jammies, read a book. It's never too early for them to get used to the sound of your voice and turning pages. Reading is as soothing to babies as it is for adults who read before bed to wind down. Books for babies and small children are very short, so this is a great step to add into your Sleep Ritual.

8 Feeding
Do what you can to keep your baby awake (tickling their feet, dressing down, etc.), as you don't want them to fall asleep while on the breast or bottle.

9 Swaddling
Once the feeding is done, lay the baby down in the bed. Newborns can't roll over because they don't yet have the muscle strength, so there is no physical need to swaddle. But almost all of the families I work with ask me to do it—often because they're scared something might happen if they don't, but also because they don't know how to put their babies down to sleep. (This will change after you start your Sleep Ritual!)

I don't give babies the tight burrito swaddle where both arms are tucked in. I prefer not to restrict their movement and give them either the right or left arm free. I also put the baby on a slight angle to prevent them from always sleeping in the same position. This helps to keep their head rounded, as opposed to having a flat back of their head. I think of a baby sleeping like a cake baking in the oven—you want to turn it a little bit to keep it nice and even.

10 Pacifiers

Pacifiers have one use and one use only: a signal to the baby to get some shut-eye. It has enormous power when it's used only for sleeping.

Babies love—and I mean LUV—that sucking motion. Toddlers do, too, so when your babies get older and realize they can have access to their beloved pacifier only when they get into bed, you can bet they're going to be jumping into bed faster than you can say peek-a-boo.

Babies are creatures of habit, so start your pacifier habit now. Any time your baby goes down for a nap or for the night, the pacifier is waiting for them in the bed. It never leaves—with one exception! The only time you can take the pacifier out of the bed is when you're going on a trip.

In other words, the pacifier is not a crutch to keep your baby happy and soothed when they're awake. But it can be a great support to help them fall asleep. Ignore anyone who tells you it's bad for your baby's teeth—a one-month-old infant doesn't have any teeth! No baby who loves that pacifier is still going to be sucking on it when they go off to college.

When you do need to go out with the baby and you know a nap is coming, be prepared. Always pack more than one pacifier (remember, they should be different colors) because you can't sterilize one if you drop it or the baby spits it out. You already know they'll do that every time you don't have a backup!

11 Lights Out and Time for Sleep

By now, your baby should be so relaxed that they will literally pass out. Don't let them fall fully asleep until they're in the bed. This can be hard at first, but do your best to keep them up so they realize that bed + pacifier = sleep.

Timing the Nighttime Sleep Ritual

Since you can't give your baby a bath until the cord finally falls off (also allowing time for the wound to close completely), you won't be able to add in the bath portion of the Nighttime Sleep Ritual for about twenty days.

You want the Ritual to be all done by 8:00 p.m. at the latest. Honestly, there's nothing an infant or a newborn needs to be doing past that time, anyway. There's nothing you need to be doing as a new parent past that time—except sleeping when the baby sleeps!

Your baby will be feeding every two and a half to three hours for breast-feeding or every three to four hours for bottle-feeding. Try to arrange your evening feed between 5:00 and 6:00 p.m. The baby will have a nap after this feeding. Yes, a baby will zonk out after every feeding. This particular one is crucial because you are training them for bedtime in the future.

If the baby has trouble sleeping, run over your checklist (gas issues, ounces drank, sleeping in an overstimulating environment). A very loud sound such as a dog barking repeatedly, loud music, or slamming doors can jolt the baby and either wake them up or keep them up the same way these sounds affect you. Yes, you want your baby to adapt and sleep in an everyday environment, but too much noise will hinder their sleep.

If nothing is working, turn off your cell phone and the lights, lay the baby comfortably on your chest, and take long, deep breaths so you are not in emotional overdrive. Breathe deeply and evenly. Relax. Allow your baby to feel your slow, even heartbeat, which will lull them right to sleep.

Babies Do Not Sleep Through the Night!

It really bothers me when parents tell me their baby is sleeping through the night—they're not! In my opinion, even a baby who goes to sleep at 11:00 p.m. and gets up at 4:00 a.m. is not sleeping through the night—but they are headed in a positive direction.

This puts undue pressure on parents dealing with sleep deprivation and worrying that their baby will never be able to sleep for long stretches. Newborns and small infants can't sleep through the night because their stomachs are so little and their fat stores so limited that they need the nutrition provided by constant, regular feeding.

Perhaps babies will stay asleep one night every few weeks for one reason or another, but they still need regular feedings. They will be having growth spurts, and their teeth will start to emerge. The best foundation you can give your baby now is an unchanging Nighttime Sleep Ritual, signaling the need to go down smoothly and quickly. As they get bigger and eat enough food to last through the night, you will be so happy you put all this work into establishing such a satisfying routine.

NAP TIME

Nap time and nighttime sleep are not quite the same. Naps come after a feeding and don't need to follow the Nighttime Sleep Ritual. Go to one of your feeding stations and relax. Don't let the baby fall asleep during the feed. Dim the lights; you don't need to darken the room entirely. Keep the TV off and put on some classical music or soft jazz from your playlist. You're aiming to let your baby know that this soothing music + feeding time = nap time afterward. Your baby is smart; they will realize music and your full attention means a nice meal and then a blissful nap. Win-win for you both.

By month 4, the baby should be down to two good naps a day. This means more awake time, and more playtime, for you both!

How to Know When It's Time for a Nap

+ Infants last two to three hours before it's TKO lights out! If you push them beyond that time frame, they will be reading you the riot act.

+ Infants do have a sleep cry. Don't worry; you will learn it. You can literally time it around every two hours.

+ Keep in mind that if they did not sleep well the night before, they will want to catch up the next day.

+ A good nap can range anywhere from one and a half to three hours. After three hours, you should start opening the door to the room and any shades so they can slowly wake up on their own.

Avoiding Cat Naps

Cats fall asleep, wake for a few minutes, and just like that, they're sleeping again. Well, that's what we don't want. If that's what you find is happening, run through this checklist:

+ Did you get a champion burp before you put them down? They could be fussy from gas.

+ Check the swaddle. If they're not swaddled, re-swaddle.

+ If they have been down for twenty minutes and are still

crying, cover them with a light blanket. Don't pick them up; just pat them on their bottom in a slow, steady rhythm. You can also hum or say something soothing in their ear.

✦ If they up the ante on the crying, it's ninja time. Be very quiet, and quickly but gently scoop them up and sit in a nice quiet place patting their back.

If they are still flexing their vocals, give them a bottle and a good burp and go for round 2.

WHAT TO DO WHEN YOUR BABY CRIES AND CRIES INSTEAD OF GOING TO SLEEP

Babies cry. That's their job! They can't open their mouths and recite the Constitution or tell you the diaper is wet and bugging them. You hear that noise? That's the only way your baby is going to tell you they're tired, hungry, y'all are talking too loud, or a noise startled them. The crying means something is up, and the baby wants the situation fixed.

That's normal crying you will very soon begin to recognize— because you'll be hearing it every day. The feeding times are going to be your milestones for knowing what the I Am Hungry cry sounds like. That cry will be slightly different from the I Am Wet and I Pooped cry, the I Don't Want to Lie Down in This Position cry, or the I Am Stressed and in Pain cry. (When you can see their larynx working, that's a good indication of a stress/pain/hurt cry.)

A newborn's cry will usually end much quicker than an infant's, which will in turn end much quicker than a toddler's. The older they get, the more these little ones realize they get attention when they cry. If you cut the crying off at the knees with a newborn, you've just saved yourself hours and hours of misery as your baby gets older. Babies are smart. They learn that if they cry because they need something and that something gets attended to, there is no longer any need to cry.

Sometimes, though, babies just cry for seemingly no reason. They cry and cry and cry, to the point where you want to cry because you're like, "WTH am I doing wrong?"—especially when you've done everything right and completed the Nighttime Sleep Ritual and faithfully given the baby gas drops. In these circumstances, though, how do you get your baby to stop crying?

The best and most important thing you need to have when putting a crying baby to sleep is patience. I know this is not what you want to read right now, but it's a fact. I've taken care of more babies than I can count, and I am prepared for anything and everything. Yet there have been plenty of times (usually in the wee hours) when the babies have started to cry and just didn't feel like stopping. Here's what you do:

+ Don't panic. Remember they feel your fear!

+ Tell yourself the baby will stop crying eventually, because this too shall pass.

+ Breathe slowly and evenly to calm yourself and lower your blood pressure and heart rate.

+ Get out a burp cloth and put it on your chest.

+ Sit down in your favorite comfy chair.

+ Put the baby on your chest and just sit there, stroking their back. Don't rock or sway back and forth—just stroke.

The goal is to make the baby feel like the two of you have become one, which is why you shouldn't rock; it's too stimulating. You want the baby to know that you are okay. When the baby feels you relaxing and can listen to your steady heartbeat, they'll calm down.

Humming also helps. It's a calming vibration. I love to hum

hymns and my favorite church songs. They soothe me while they soothe the baby. Jessica Biel was really funny because she'd walk out of the room and ask me what song I was humming because she wanted to hum the same one. I'd tell her it was "Yes, Jesus Loves Me" or "Mary, Don't You Weep."

A baby who is on a regular schedule will cry when the schedule is interrupted. This cry can quickly turn into ear-shattering screaming, especially if the baby is hungry or overstimulated. I see this happen all the time in church, and it's not the baby's fault. Parents should not be bringing the baby somewhere during feeding or nap time if there are easy alternatives (like going to a church service earlier or later in the day).

Stop and think before you make plans. Your world now revolves around your baby and their schedule. The most important thing you can do right now is feed your baby well so they get good, restful sleep, and then feed yourself well so you can get good, restful sleep. That's it. If you try to cram it all in and your foundation isn't settled, there will be problems that will just become worse when you go back to work. You will be more exhausted at the end of the day, and the baby will be able to sense your stress and start crying. The last thing I ever want you to do is set yourself up for failure.

chapter nine

PLAYTIME WITH BABY

Justin Timberlake and Jessica Biel: "Nanny Connie taught us the importance of black and white colors for the baby's developing brain. She wore a hospital scrub dotted with black and white cows, and we watched our tiny infant stare mesmerized at those cows for months. And I'm not kidding you, but that boy has an affinity for those animals over any other and a fat ole brain to match. By watching and listening to Connie, we learned how important it is to talk to your infant. All the time. Tell them what you're doing, even if it feels ridiculous. Our kid's vocabulary is outrageous now. He said 'condensation' and 'tornado' at one and a half. Thank you, Nanny!"

A lot of new parents think playtime is just about toys, but it actually starts as soon as the baby comes home. It's not just fun for your little one—it's really fun for you, and a wonderful taste of all the games and playing you'll be engaged in when the baby gets older.

Your little bean spent nine months living in a snug and warm cocoon. Then, all of a sudden, there are some heavy-duty pushes and a strange journey through a narrow passage, only to emerge in a bright, clanging room filled with strange sounds and smells. Who wouldn't cry with the shock of it!

What does the birth process have to do with playtime? Well, newborns are basically blind and can navigate only through smelling and hearing, which are very well developed at birth. You need to get close to your baby and let them smell and hear you. Once they're a few weeks older and can see a bit better and smell a lot better, they will start tracking your scent from one side of the room to another and connecting your voice to it.

Think of this first month as a classroom for newborns. You're literally training your child to respond to you.

Your baby already knows you and wants to interact in whatever way they can.

Playtime starts now!

Of course, this means anyone who is regularly in the house with the baby—your partner, the baby's siblings, caregivers, or your friends—should be ready for playtime, too.

TALKING IS THE BEST TOY YOUR BABY NEEDS RIGHT NOW

You can never talk too much to your baby—unless it's the end of your Nighttime Sleep Ritual. Your conversation can be as simple as telling them about your day. Talk to your baby just like you talk to your friends. They won't understand any of the words yet, but they will understand your tone of voice—and that's the trick. Your voice should be playful.

Once you realize that talking is the equivalent of playing for a baby, it will become much easier for you to talk in a playful way, and then the talking will turn into games when the baby is a little bit older.

Parents often ask me why their voices instinctively go up higher when they're speaking to babies, and it's because higher tones are easier to hear. While in utero, everything your baby heard was muffled and indistinct. It's pretty amazing that your body knows that a higher tone will be easier for your baby to process. That doesn't mean you should speak in gibberish or baby talk— only that you go up a few notes on the scale until you can see that your baby is paying attention.

Even if you're not having the best day, talk to your baby. If you are stressed or anxious, pay attention to your baby's face and body language. This will help you calm yourself and go back to your usual sweet voice that your baby already loves so well.

Talking as playtime not only teaches your child about fun, but it will also help improve your baby's vocabulary.

Reading to your baby is also playtime. Don't just read the book—act out the voices and make up your own stories to go along with their picture books. That's fun for you both and will become a wonderful habit. Soft books are great because babies can safely teethe on them. You should start reading to your baby as soon as the baby is home from the hospital!

Don't underestimate how much your baby knows already. I love when parents crack up from the looks and the side-eyes they get from their babies. There's a scene I love in the movie *The Fifth Element* that reminds me of how infants learn to talk. Milla Jovovich's character is an alien in an adult body, and she has to learn how to speak in English. She sits in front of a TV for an extended period, and after she reaches the tipping point, she goes, "Okay, I'm programmed," and just starts talking. That's what babies do. They hear voices, they listen, and then all of a sudden, they can make sounds and words, and from that moment on, they'll be talking as much as you!

By month 2, your baby is going to get it. During that first month, I like to think they're still talking to their buddies in heaven. Those funny little half-smiles you see—that's babies getting their last little giggles with their old friends before they leave them behind and fully engage with you. The first time you see your baby start to track you and pull a genuine, Hey-I-know-you-you-always-have-the-best-snacks smile, your heart will melt into a puddle of pure love.

THINK IN BLACK AND WHITE

I'm sure you never thought something as simple as the color of your skin would be so impactful on your infant's development, but it is! As I said, newborns are basically blind when they come into the world. They can't focus yet, and their eye muscles are very weak. Your baby will only see in black and white for the first five to six months, so one way to help them start putting a face to the voice they've been hearing for nine months is to wear colors that contrast with your skin tone. If your skin is fair, wear darker colors; if your skin is dark, wear lighter colors. It's that simple!

In the very beginning of my baby-nursing career, my parents would be in awe of their infants tracking me across the room or connecting with me as I hovered over the mother when she breast-fed. There I was, this melanin-rich woman in a white uniform basically looking like a billboard to the newborns. Parents would start asking, "How can I get my infant to follow my hand the way they are following yours?" Or, "Why is my infant so connected to you when you wave your fingers?"

I would give them simple exercises, such as wearing a

dark-colored glove on their white hand, or vice versa, and waving it very slowly from left to right. I would also have them dig through their drawers to find a contrasting-colored T-shirt and then sit down and have a conversation with the baby. This helped the voice their infant heard for the past nine months start to take the shape of their parent.

Everything you do with your infant from the first moment they come into the world is a teaching moment.

Mobiles

What's the one thing your baby sees more than you? No, not your iPad. Their mobile.

Many parents see mobiles as cute decorations rather than essential developmental tools, but they are so much more than that. They are the visual equivalent of your baby's first book.

The best mobiles are black and white, mirrored, and shiny, with a lot of movement. There's no such thing as having too many mobiles, and you should place them wherever you can put one: the changing table, bassinet, crib, bouncy seat, and car seat.

Black and white color-contrasting doesn't just stop with you. I know it's tempting to choose a mobile that has all the colors of the rainbow, but it's better to choose function over fashion. Stick to black and white for now. Your little one is going to find this mobile more entertaining than a colorful one because it's something they can see clearly. This will be their first lesson that learning is fun, and you will love watching your baby start tracking an object.

If you don't find a mobile you like in a store, it's ridiculously easy to make your own. All you need to do is hang anything that's black and white: white Styrofoam balls from a craft store, decorated with black markers or covered in black-and-white patterned cloth. String them and hang them securely—that's the most important step, as you don't want the mobile to fall on the baby.

These mobiles will have a huge payoff when your baby is about five or six months old and is delighted to play with the black-and-white toys you introduced when they were newborns. It's an amazing thing to see.

Rotate Those Toys and Stuffed Animals!

Although your baby is still too young to have any stuffed animals or toys to play with, I know you've already got a collection larger than the shelves at Build-A-Bear. If you want to display the animals or other toys, go right ahead. My trick is to rotate them every few weeks. Out of sight means out of mind for little ones, so they'll think they're getting a brand-new toy if they haven't seen it for a while. You better believe this is going to save you buckets when your baby gets old enough to turn on the waterworks when you say no in the toy store.

Massage Is a Great Way to Play

You already know how important it is to give your baby a massage after their warm and cozy bath. Think of yourself as your baby's personal trainer. Except the massage isn't a workout—it's playtime!

Place your baby in the middle of a firm bed so you don't have to worry about them falling off. Gently stroke those little fingers and start your monologue. Then bicycle their little legs to help their joints. Doing this will help you incorporate playtime into your daily baby-care schedule, which is really important. Add nursery rhymes and silly songs to your massage time. Go for some tickling, too. You can never have too much fun!

chapter ten

TIME TO TAKE BABY OUTSIDE

Matt Damon and John Krasinski: Matt and John certainly did their homework to make sure they were prepared. Matt was a manual reader. While most men would just look at the pictures, Matt was focused on reading all the instructions to make sure all the safety requirements were met. Now, John, he was a visual learner. He could take the Pack 'n Play up and down, change a diaper, and know when the bottle temperature was just right, all without breaking a sweat! When his friends came over to visit, he showed up and showed out!

It can be nerve-wracking for all new parents to take their precious little bundles outside into the big, bad world, but with a few trips under your belt, you'll gain all the confidence you need.

Here's my best tip: Keep your eyes on the clock. Do not leave if it's close to feeding time.

BE PROTECTIVE OF YOUR BABY

Now, I know the majority of parents don't have *TMZ* chasing them down. But I've been in those situations, and it's taught me super-woman-level efficiency when going out with my babies. Here's how to protect your little one while you're out and about. (Trust me, this list is how I've survived the past thirty years.)

+ Stock your car and your stroller with a survival kit that includes gas drops, an extra bottle, water and snacks (for you), diapers, and wipes.

+ Before you leave the house, plan what you'll be carrying. Put as much stuff as you can in the car before the baby goes in. You never want to go to the car with your arms full—you can easily lose your balance, and the baby will go tumbling down with you. Your baby is the only thing you should be carrying when you make your last trip to the car.

+ If your baby starts crying in the car, pull over in the nearest parking lot and see what the issue is. Make sure it is a safe area, lock your doors, roll your windows up, and turn the air on if it's hot. Always get into the backseat with Baby and never stand outside your car.

+ Use a swaddle cloth or thin blanket (muslin works great) to drape over the handle of the carrier when outside. Then pull the visor up so the swaddle stays on top of it. This is great for when it's super-sunny or even raining outside. The baby will be safe and protected. The swaddle is thin and breathable, so don't stress about whether they can breathe. Then snap the carrier into the base of the car seat and pull back the visor.

+ Pick a stroller where the baby faces you. This will help protect you from strangers approaching your baby without your permission. By month 4, if your baby's neck muscles are strong enough, using a sling is also a great way to protect the baby. Make sure to pick a sling with head and neck protection, and read the warnings/instructions very carefully to prevent accidental suffocation.

Getting Stressed When You're Out with the Baby

As a new parent, you have a lot of love, anxiety, and protectiveness flooding through you, which makes you hypersensitive to stress. At this point anything can take you from 0–100 real quick when you have your baby in tow—from the driver who cuts you off to the cashier who has an attitude about doing their job to the complete stranger who rubs their germ-infested hand over your baby's face. To minimize this stress, you'll have to be confident carrying around the baby.

Practice walking around with the carrier before the baby is born. It's a bulky object that isn't easy to maneuver. Put a few heavy books or cans of food in it so you can get used to the weight, then walk around with it in the house or take it out for a stroll. Get comfortable with this new appendage being on the outside of your body as opposed to being on the inside. Then when you're out with the baby, you're already more mindful and physically confident about the little bean you're carrying.

After the baby comes, you'll want to practice all the scenarios again at home. You want to be on point when you're in a parking lot at the grocery store or at lunch with your friends.

Set Up Boundaries When You're Out with the Baby

You will soon find out that most people are very nice and just love to coo over babies. Who wouldn't? But never feel that you have to let anyone get near your baby when you don't want them to. This is especially important with newborns and tiny infants who haven't received their shots yet and whose immune systems are only starting to get revved up. The last thing you need is a stranger with a cold sneezing in your baby's face.

Set up your boundaries for how you let anyone approach you when you're out with the baby. Throw the swaddle or lightweight blanket over the carrier, which serves as a notice that the baby isn't available at the moment. If strangers don't get the hint, let them know you have an infant who isn't vaccinated. If they still continue to push, don't bite your tongue! Let them know in no uncertain terms that they aren't getting their germy hands anywhere near your child. However, most people get the hint when the carrier is covered, so explanations shouldn't be necessary.

Bottom line: You do not owe anyone anything.

It's easy for me to teach this to my families because I am the designated pit bull. I have zero qualms about setting and enforcing boundaries. I am not a permanent member of my families, so the dynamic is different for me. I've lost count of how many parents have confided that they were scared of their mothers-in-law but didn't know how to tell them not to wear perfume or show off the baby to everyone in church.

Discuss your boundaries and wishes with your family, friends, and caregivers before you go out with the baby. This will make it easier for you to manage the people you'll meet when you run your errands or take your baby to church, where you might run into people you know. Most strangers are parents themselves and will understand where you're coming from and respect you for it.

BABY'S GOT A BUG: TIME TO TAKE
THE BABY TO THE DOCTOR

Always try to book the first appointment in the morning or the first appointment after lunch, so you will have less time to wait in case other patients are running late. Be sure to explain to the receptionist that you are coming with a newborn, so you won't have to sit in the waiting room with sick children.

I have found making a list of things you have tried at home helps you to get a better result when speaking with your doctor. They are on a time limit, so giving the doctor this list will get you a solution much more quickly and efficiently.

If You Adopted

If you are adopting, try to get as much information about the medical histories of the biological parents as you can. This isn't always possible (especially with international adoptions), but do your best. There is an added level of fear of the unknown when your child doesn't share the DNA of you and your partner, but the love and affection is the same, and that's what really matters.

First Doctor's Visit

The baby's initial checkup will take place in the first two weeks. This is basically just a general look to make sure the baby is eating well, that you're okay, and to answer any questions. You will also likely be given a follow-up schedule for vaccinations and other wellness checkups.

When going to your first doctor visit, prepare your diaper bag the night before (don't forget your log journal!), and if you have questions, write them down before you go, as you're liable to forget!

Ask About a Well Room Before You Go

Many pediatricians have separate rooms for well visits and for babies and children who are sick or have a rash. If you know your doctor doesn't have a well room, call ahead and say you're coming in with a newborn so you can immediately be put in an exam room and not sit in the larger waiting room with everyone else and expose your baby to their germs.

It's okay to be a little overprotective—paranoid, even—at the doctor's office. I know how adorable your baby is and how you want to show them off, but doctors' offices are like Petri dishes, especially in winter when everyone seems to have a cold or the flu. Keep your baby in the carrier facing you and hang the swaddle on top for extra protection.

When to Call the Doctor

You don't want to become the kind of parent who calls the doctor for every minor issue (like gas!), but you also don't want to feel like a bother and not call when there's a problem.

✦ Trust your intuition. Even after a week or two, you're going to have an excellent handle on your baby's habits. If there's a change in their poop or how much they're feeding, or if they are suddenly fussy or just seem off, call the doctor.

✦ If your baby seems warm, take their temperature and write down the symptoms and the time you first noticed them so you won't forget when you call the doctor. Fevers over 100.3

degrees Fahrenheit in such a young baby are emergencies, so call your doctor immediately.

+ Febrile seizures are seizures accompanied by a fever above 100.3 and are common and rarely life-threatening, though they're terrifying for parents. They usually happen in children from three months to six years old. Call 911 first, then your doctor. You don't know what is going to happen next, and you never want to drive with a sick baby. The ambulance can get you to a hospital and begin treatment more quickly.

+ I've had moms put kids down for bed with a very slight fever, and when they went in to check on them, the baby was having a febrile seizure. By the time the mom called 911, I would already be in the kitchen getting the ice into the sink to prepare a cool bath. (Never put a baby in an ice bath—dropping the temperature too rapidly can also induce a seizure.) This is exactly what the 911 operator would tell them to do, but it's always better to ask for help if you have any doubts.

+ An unresponsive or limp baby is also an emergency. Call 911 immediately. Then call your pediatrician.

COMMON AILMENTS AND HOW TO TREAT THEM

These are some of the most common medical conditions that can be treated at home.

Jaundice

Neonatal jaundice is fairly common in babies around the thirty-seventh or thirty-eighth week of pregnancy. This happens when the baby's liver is not mature enough to get rid of the excess bilirubin (a pigment made during the breakdown of red blood cells) in the bloodstream. Jaundice can show up in babies as early as seventy-two hours after birth.

The higher the bilirubin number, the more severe the jaundice. A normal bilirubin count usually ranges from 0 to 7; a range from 7 to 12 needs medical treatment. While this is very stressful and can bring any parent to tears thinking they have done something wrong, trust me, you haven't; your baby just needs a little help getting that liver on track.

Eagle-eyed parents will notice jaundice sooner. You may think your beautiful infant is a great sleeper in those first few days because all they do is conk out, or you may think their yellow skin tone is going to be a phenomenal color. Well, those are two red flags. The third red flag is if you prick their heel very gently with a needle and the baby doesn't cry immediately.

The best thing to do is place that baby in front of the window, in direct sunlight, for short periods so they can get their vitamin D through the quickest route, their belly button. There's nothing wrong with Mother Nature giving you a helping hand!

Also make sure the baby gets plenty of liquids by offering them a bottle every two hours. It is harder to keep jaundiced babies awake during feedings, because their little livers need to get flushed, which happens during deep sleep. As soon as the jaundice improves, the baby will get on a normal sleep cycle. Do whatever you can to keep the baby up—tickle their feet, strip off their clothes, or move into a chillier room.

Your pediatrician will also be on top of this when you go in for that first well-baby checkup. It's also important to monitor your jaundiced baby's weight, pee, and poopy diapers in the first few weeks, as they tend to sleep so much that they don't get enough feedings or fluids in.

Some doctors' offices will give you an ultraviolet light or a little glow worm as a treatment if you are in an area where there is low sunlight or the days are short. A bilirubin belt, or bed, is like a tanning bed for infants, and doctors usually send a consultant to your home to assist you in setup and usage. Your baby will have to be in the belt or bed for a significant amount of time for a couple of days. The longer the baby is there, the better.

You can also monitor your baby's progress by simply pressing your thumb on their skin. The longer it takes your fingerprint to disappear, the higher the bilirubin count. Other signs of recovery are being more vocal and sleeping less. The skin will become pinkish or flesh-toned and the whites of the eyes pearly. There will be an increase in wet diapers, and their stool diapers should change in color and consistency depending on what milk they are fed.

In my experience, jaundice almost always happens within the first three weeks, and there is little chance of reoccurrence. When your baby is crying, kicking, pooping, screaming, and lacking in the sleep department—congratulations! Things are on track now.

I learned all about this on one of my more memorable journeys early in my baby-nurse career, with Little Miss Turner Spotswood, whose bilirubin count was in the teens. We went to the hospital twelve times; literally, we had to go every day to get her bilirubin count checked. I learned the importance of the ranges and expectation goals, and I realized I would have to step up my game and study this process to lessen both the mother's and my stress of sitting in the hospital lab with a newborn.

Thrush

Thrush can happen as long as the baby is drinking milk. It is caused by yeast in their mouth that forms from milk settling in the crevices of their cheeks and looks like tiny white ulcers or blisters. The best way to prevent it is by not allowing a baby to fall asleep with milk bottles in their mouths.

If your baby has thrush, don't use the same nipple twice and boil your bottle nipples to kill bacteria. If you're breast-feeding, clean your bras frequently. I recommend Dreft detergent to reduce bacteria. You should also change your breast pads frequently during the day. If the pad is saturated, clean your breast prior to replacing the pad or feeding the baby. This is especially important on warm days because you can transfer bacteria from your breast to your baby's mouth.

Pediatricians sometimes prescribe a purple stain called gentian violet. Gently swab the infected areas with cotton after every feeding. (Caution: This will stain everything.) You'll probably need to use it religiously for a couple of weeks. You might also be prescribed Diflucan or Nystatin, which are buttercream in color and work similarly to gentian violet but without the staining.

Skin Issues

So many babies are born with less-than-perfect skin, and it's absolutely nothing to worry about. They're shedding a whole layer of skin that kept them protected from the amniotic fluid.

Baby soaps tend to dry out babies' skin, so I searched for lotions that retain the moisture and help with the rough spots some babies have. I suggest using Lubriderm Sensitive Skin, shea butter, Cetaphil, and Aveeno. Put it on their arms, legs, and body, but, as you know, never on the hands. Remember that your makeup, perfume, colognes, aftershave, detergents, creams, and even lipsticks can cause allergic reactions or skin irritation. Fragrance-free products are a must at this time. You should expect to see improvements in your baby's skin around the second week.

Cradle Cap

Cradle cap is a gummy scab buildup at the base of the hair follicle. It is not normal dandruff and will look worse if you pick at it, so please don't! The cause of cradle cap is unknown, but some think it might have to do with an overproduction of oil in the hair follicles.

If your baby has cradle cap, use the soft surgical brush you should have gotten in the hospital. If you didn't get one, try a mushroom brush with very soft bristles. Cradle the baby's head in your hand and scrub it all over with the brush in circular or back-and-forth motions, starting with the fontanel in the back and up to the front of the baby's head. You can also use a tiny dab of organic, unscented baby shampoo on the brush. Follow that with an application of a little bit of organic olive oil, coconut oil, or shea butter and rub it in gently with your fingers.

After about a month of this gentle scrub treatment, the cradle cap usually disappears for good.

Heat Rash

Heat can cause your baby's skin to break out in a rash or pimples. The more folds a baby has, the more sweat they collect, which leads to an excess of skin bacteria. Cornstarch is a great drying agent to absorb the moisture. Use a large makeup brush to dust the baby's crevices and keep clothing to a minimum so the skin can air out. Avoid using talc-based powders, which are rarely pure, or baby powder, which is not absorbent, cakes up, and causes irritation.

Babies need to be protected from the harsh sunrays, but chemical sunscreens can't be used on babies under the age of six months. Discuss with your pediatrician whether you can use mineral sunscreens, which contain zinc oxide as physical blockers. In the meantime, keep the baby out of the sun, use the visor on the carrier, get hoods for the stroller, and give yourself permission to buy a devastatingly cute wardrobe of sunhats!

Hot Spots

Many babies develop these rough patches of skin that, if severe, can crack and bleed slightly, on their arms or legs. There are three reasons why they occur: genetics, soap or skin care products that cause dryness, and hard water. If you haven't started using Cetaphil, get some now and apply it several times a day on the patches. Continue to wash the baby's clothing in Dreft detergent. You should see improvement within ten days of using Cetaphil; if not, discuss more advanced treatment with your pediatrician.

Vaccinations

We all want to protect our kids, and you have to do what you think is best as a parent. Whether you decide to vaccinate or not, you need to do your research and speak with your pediatrician. There are risks no matter what you decide, and you need to be prepared for those scenarios.

The dreaded needles come out at two months, followed by boosters at four months (except for hepatitis B, which is given at birth, if needed).

It will be hard to see your baby hurting from the surprise and the pain of the needle. You can massage the baby's thighs with rubbing alcohol or witch hazel before the shots, and doing this afterward as well can help with soreness. As tempting as it is to give your baby a painkiller beforehand, no baby can be given ibuprofen or any other form of painkiller until they are six months old, unless you have gotten permission from your pediatrician.

Before going in for your shot visit, ask your pediatrician if there are any illnesses going around, as your baby's immune system will be more vulnerable after multiple vaccinations.

Be prepared for irritable nights. If you or anyone in your family is feeling under the weather or just getting over being sick, they should stay away from the baby. Since you can't *not* handle your baby, avoid breathing on them as much as possible (use a medical face mask if you're sick) and wash your hands frequently with hot, soapy water. Get your hands clean—don't just get your germs wet! This means a vigorous scrubbing.

part four

OPERATION MANUAL
FOR PARENTS

chapter eleven

TAKING CARE OF YOUR PHYSICAL NEEDS

Jessica Biel: "Connie introduced me to the real meaning of grits. Good to note that grits are not the same as Cream of Wheat. They are actually corn. She made blackened chicken, roast, pork chops, ribs, yards and yards of filet, greens, spinach, green beans, potatoes, and it goes on. Pound cake, strawberry cake, cupcakes, German chocolate cake, cornbread, biscuits. It was truly the greatest eating experience of my whole life and my friends' lives who were lucky enough to be over on the days that the Southern aromas wafted out of the kitchen and into our sad little West Coast nasal cavities. Thanks, Nanny!"

Taking the best possible care of your baby isn't just about feedings, changings, bath time, and a sleep ritual. It's all about you, too. The best way to take care of your new little one is to take care of yourself—physically and emotionally.

Almost every mom I've worked with has wildly underestimated the physical toll the birth process took on her body. Back when I was growing up, women spent at least four to five days and sometimes a week in the hospital with their newborns, getting the rest they needed without having to worry about physical baby care other than feedings. Now, new moms who have vaginal births leave the hospital after only a day or two. Of course, you'll want to get back to the familiar comfort of your home with your precious bundle, but doing so before you're physically ready can prolong your recovery.

Your body has been through trauma, and you need at least six weeks to recuperate after a vaginal birth, and perhaps longer if you had a C-section. Take it easy. Don't push yourself.

You know why? A hard head makes a soft ass! I can't tell you the number of times I've said, "God bless you" to the mothers who run home and try to turn into Superwoman. "I got this," they say as they completely forget to care for themselves . . . then fall apart.

As mothers, we are wired to conquer it all, but we are no good to our children if we don't take care of ourselves. I thoroughly go over my list of Dos and Don'ts with moms after they arrive home from the hospital: sleep when the baby sleeps, don't lift heavy things, and stay off your feet.

EATING FOR TWO

One of your top concerns, obviously, is shedding the baby weight. That last trimester is so brutal on a mom's body. You were bloated and enormous, and the last thing you want to do after the baby finally pops out is to look down and wonder when your cankles will turn back into your ankles.

I see you in the supermarket. You pick out a pile of fresh greens and tell yourself that salads are healthy (well, yes, they are!). You swap the bagels for English muffins, you cut back on cheese, and you ignore your tummy rumbling.

Let me save you before you buy the kale: if you're going to be breast-feeding, banish the word *diet* from your vocabulary. You need to up your nutrient intake and consume more calories because your body needs more energy to produce breast milk. Instead of thinking about what you shouldn't eat to lose the baby weight, you should be asking yourself, "What should I add today?"

Fat is your new BFF. Formula already has all the fats added, but if you're breast-feeding, only you can ensure your milk is as nutritious as possible—and that means fatty. My daddy always told me quality over quantity, and that notion applies to your milk. You can produce enough milk to fill a walk-in freezer, but if your milk is lacking, you just made some very interesting ice packs. Breast-feeding is one half production and one half quality. Breast milk that isn't rich enough will have your baby on formula quicker than a fly on a donkey's ass.

I've had some stern talking-tos with moms who were busy fussing about breast-feeding, the right environment, and all-organic food. I told them it doesn't matter how fresh and organic the food is if they're calorie counting.

If you're not eating good food and getting enough calories, you will always have crappy milk. It'll be mostly water with little nutritional value. Thinking your breast milk will be fantastically nourishing when you're not nourishing yourself is magical thinking.

Go for the gusto, girl! I am giving you total permission to not only eat right, but to eat for two. If you don't, your baby is going to be the one who pays for it, and I know you don't want that to happen.

My Favorite Foods for Breast-feeding Moms

Do you know how many nutrition classes medical students take in medical school? One, if they're lucky. (Ask your doctor if you don't believe me!) As a result, you can't count on your obstetrician or pediatrician to give you detailed advice about what you should or shouldn't eat. They'll just follow the government guidelines on the food pyramid while encouraging you to "eat right," "eat better," and "make sure you're eating enough."

Enough? What does that mean? It means you're still in your fourth trimester. You're going to be nurturing your baby with all the great food you're going to be eating, with the same care and diligence you spent in the previous three trimesters.

Home Cooking Is Best

I grew up in a house of fantastic cooks who could work magic on a simple chicken, so I am always shocked when some of my families don't know how to boil water. Cooking is a skill every parent should have because you'll need to cook for your kids as they get older, and it's ridiculously easy and also very stress relieving once you master the basics. You'll not only be in complete charge of what goes into your body, but you'll save buckets of money. If you're not confident in the kitchen, have a friend come over and walk you through a few meals while you're feeding the baby.

This is really important for all moms, especially breast-feeders. Cooking for yourself is the only way to monitor your intake, because there's no way to know what other cooks put in their dishes. Packaged foods are labeled, but you won't know the exact quantities of any added chemicals, preservatives, or artificial flavors or colors you're ingesting.

If you're a junk-food junkie, you don't want to go cold turkey on the way you eat, but you also need to be mindful of what you're putting in your body because your baby is eating whatever you're eating. I understand that life happens and sometimes you just need to go through a drive-thru. There's no judgment! Just try not to make it a habit. My motto is "Fresh is best," so if you can't spell it or pronounce it, you might want to pass on it! You don't have to be Julia Child every meal, but peanut butter and jelly isn't going to make the mark either. Something as simple as pork tenderloin with a loaded baked potato and spinach or green beans (one of my go-to meals for breast-feeding mothers) is a great choice for dinner. Add a slice of buttered French bread on the side, and you will have a meal in less than forty-five minutes.

You need good, nutrient-dense meals, meaning a balance of good fats, protein, and carbohydrates from fresh food, preferably in season and organic. Roast chicken, roasted fish (with butter), or a broiled steak and a baked potato (with butter) are perfect meals. Slow-cooker stews with some meat and cut-up, non-gassy veggies make a great no-fuss dinner. Get a slow cooker and throw the ingredients in it early in the day, and dinner will be ready with no worry hours later. You can have dessert, but do not go buck wild. Eat a lot of juicy, delicious fruit and stay away from gas-producing chocolate. Dessert is not dinner!

COOKING WITH CELEBRITY CHEF JOHN CURRENCE

The first time I met Connie Simpson was on a sweltering summer day in 1998. She thrust one of her powerful hands toward me, pulled me into her grasp, and informed me for the very first time that we were family and that "family does not shake hands; we hug."

I am a chef by trade, so food is a very easy common subject to fall into. But I was equally fascinated with the nutritional regimen Connie demands for her clients. On top of all of her other duties, she cooks for her families and cooks she does—amazing food. In our exploration of her culinary philosophy, it immediately became clear that she employed a well-researched blend of "nanny wisdom" with solid knowledge of nutritional academics. We discussed the importance of whole milk versus low-fat or skim in a mother's diet, as well as the average metabolic rates for mothers to process alcohol or spices. I loved every second of that afternoon, visiting with her in that sun-dappled den in the back of my brother Richard's house, while my sister-in-law Mathilde was resting.

As we chatted, Connie mentioned she and Mathilde had talked several times about her love for my shrimp and grits and that she had never had the dish before. Wanting to further endear myself to my new friend, I immediately volunteered to run out to the store and gather the provisions to make shrimp and grits for dinner. I think I cemented the love of both of those women in the first forkful.

Two years later, my second niece was born in Austin, Texas, and again, Connie was at the helm. Richard had informed me weeks prior to the labor and birth of their child that Connie and Mathilde had made it perfectly clear that the shrimp and grits dinner would be as integral a part of the process as the epidural and he was to make the arrangements. I came . . . I saw . . . I produced . . . again, I conquered. Connie and I cemented our friendship. I get the occasional call from Connie to ask me to come and cook for one of her clients as her gift to them, and there is never a moment of hesitation when I am given the opportunity to go somewhere and spend a few moments drawing from the bottomless well of wisdom, humor, honestly, and love that is my friend Connie Simpson. She truly is the best at what she does.

Here's to you, Connie Simpson, you make the transition in this aspect of life like slicing through soft butter. God bless you. I love you, sister.

—Celebrity Chef John Currence

Fat Is Your Friend

Good fats are unbelievably important for brain development. Did you know human brains are made up primarily of fat? Well, now you do. And your baby is not going to get fat if you eat fat! There is no way a breast-feeding mom can make her baby obese—it just isn't physically possible.

I know I keep saying you're going to be getting all these new BFFs, but butter is really going to be your new BFF. Let me share a secret with you: many of my moms thought I sprinkled their food with magic, but it was simply butter. That skillet toast was loaded with butter. So were the oatmeal and eggs. And let's not forget my famous sour cream pound cake. My recipe calls for a half-pound of butter.

I love seeing the smiles on new moms' faces when they eat some good, hot home-cooked food, with a crusty French baguette on the side, slathered in butter.

Drink full-fat milk. Eat full-fat yogurt and cheese. Chow down on avocados, olive oil, and nut oils.

But stay away from the bad fats: trans-fats, anything hydrogenated like Crisco or margarine, coconut oil, and lard—basically any fat that is totally solid at room temperature. These fats are used in most packaged and prepared foods, especially baked goods, giving you another good reason to turn on the stove yourself!

Carbohydrates Are Your Friends, Too

Carbs are not the enemy. There are good carbs, like vegetables and fruit, and there are bad carbs, like white bread, potato chips, and white table sugar. Eating whole-grain bread and grains is going to give you energy, fill you up, and make you less likely to binge on sweets or junk.

What Not to Eat While Breast-feeding

Most pediatricians and lactation consultants are rolling their eyes as they say, "This is nothing but an old wives' tale." I say, "The proof is in the pudding." Try it both ways and let me know which one works for you.

Monitoring your intake of gas-producing foods can make a huge difference in how well your baby feeds and sleeps. If these dietary restrictions have you feeling like you're stuck in your last trimester—your own personal Groundhog Day!—you'll soon see how avoiding certain foods will make your life and your baby's easier.

Good-bye Gassy Foods

It's a bit of an adjustment for moms used to eating healthy diets to cut back on many of their favorite foods, especially if they are nutrient-dense, low calorie, and full of fiber. This means that staples such as broccoli and Brussels sprouts; fermented foods like sauerkraut or pickles; fiber-rich foods like beans, figs, and sweet potatoes; and highly spiced foods are off the menu.

You should start off very bland (a carb, a protein, and a non-gassy vegetable such as spinach, squash, or green beans, etc.), seasoned only with salt and pepper. The Hell, No List consists of leftovers (gas builds up in leftover foods, so anything over one night is pushing the envelope), cabbage, caffeine, chocolate, nuts, broccoli, lentils, bell peppers, hot peppers, and highly seasoned foods.

When figuring out how well your baby tolerates what you've eaten, you can always add, but you can't take away. In other words, it will take your body/breasts between twenty-four and forty-eight hours to process what you ate, and you won't know your baby's response to the milk until then. It's better to have plain mashed potatoes as opposed to glorified mashed potatoes, or a steak with just a little salt on it to see how the baby does. If there's no extra gas, then maybe add a little bit of sour cream to your potatoes and a spoonful of barbecue sauce to your steak next time. This will help you manage gas and get the nutrients you both need.

Stick to simple, barely spiced food at first. This, of course, will vary by culture. A baby from India, for example, whose mom ate intensely flavored curries all her life, is not going to react to spice the way an American baby whose parents ate a blander diet would. Pay attention to your partner's food habits, too, as your baby has inherited 50 percent of his genes. If he has certain food intolerances or allergies, your baby may have them as well.

I know how tempting it is to drink a lot of coffee when you're exhausted and trying to stay awake during the day, but it's not only going to affect your sleep later that night, it is also a big gas producer. Only drink coffee or caffeinated tea before noon—giving the baby an evening jolt is not on the list. I'll bet you cut way down on coffee when you were pregnant, so try not to get back into the caffeine habit while you're breast-feeding. If you are drinking a lot of coffee, don't cold-turkey it; you can get really bad headaches. Slowly wean yourself off by increasing the percentage of decaf to regular over a period of a few weeks, and you should be fine.

Chocoholics, Beware!

If there's one food the moms I work with sneak, it would, of course, be chocolate. But who knew chocolate is one of the gassiest foods you can eat? Not my moms—until they ate it!

I went with one of my moms and her twins to the pediatrician for their two-month checkups. I told the doctor everything had been going well with the twins up until the previous night. One of the twins was inconsolable, and I had done all my checks and balances but was unsure of the exact problem. The doctor gave us some advice as Mom sat very quietly listening. As we walked back out to the car, she burst into tears.

"I had a Hershey bar last night," she said. "I'm so sorry!"

You can do it—your chocolate purgatory won't last forever. If you have a sweet tooth, it's important to avoid sugar as much as you can, but it's not realistic to deprive yourself of all the treats you love, either. Read labels. It's not so much the sugar in candy that makes gas but the artificial colors and flavors—they can really mess up your gut. If you can't spell it or pronounce it, you might want to pass on it.

Reintroducing Your Favorite Foods

By month 3, you might be out of Chocolate Jail. The more bitter (and the more antioxidants), the better. If there's a lot of gas, back to Jail for another month!

In month 4, you can very gradually start adding more foods and a bit of spice to your diet. Do this one by one so you can gauge any gassy reactions from the baby. Otherwise, you won't have any idea which food upset Baby's stomach.

How Much Breast-feeding Moms Should Drink the First Month

+ When you first start breast-feeding, you are going to be thirsty all the time, and you will make me very happy if you're guzzling water all day long.

+ One of the best things you can do for yourself and the baby when you're breast-feeding is drink a lot of water. Like, a lot—almost two gallons. (Make sure you have a visual of your intake so you can see yourself accomplishing your goal.) No sweeteners, no fizz, no soda—just plain old water. Flavor it if you like with a little lemon, orange, or even rosemary or other herbs—whatever you want to put in it to make it more digestible.

✦ Avoid seltzer and all sodas. What creates the carbonation? Dreaded gas, of course! Also, if you've had a C-section, the bubbles and gas will give you cramps.

The Pump and Dump

Do you like beer? Good. Because your baby is going to like it when you drink beer. Not light beer—nonalcoholic dark beer. It's yeasty and oh so good for you. (The yeast helps with milk production, and the darker the beer, the more yeast it has.) My breast-feeding moms are ecstatic when I tell them they can drink two or three cans a day.

If you go out to dinner and have a cocktail or go over to a friend's house and have a small glass of red wine with your meal, it will be a pump-and-dump night. My go-to plan for moms who want to go out and drink alcohol is:

✦ Express your milk before you go out.

✦ Take your pump with you.

✦ Have one drink, preferably red wine or dark beer.

✦ Drink a lot of water. As in, a lot of water.

✦ If you're going to have this drink at 8:00 p.m. and you're still out three hours later, do a good pumping and dump the milk.

✦ The next feeding will be totally fine for the baby.

✦ Do not feel guilty about having an occasional drink. Just pump and dump.

GETTING A (GENTLE) MOVE ON:
THE EXERCISE YOU NEED

When Will the Weight Really Start to Come Off?

Most new moms think breast-feeding will automatically help them lose weight. But breast-feeding helps take the weight off because most moms don't put in enough calories—not because it makes them masters of the metabolism universe!

Load up those plates and be prepared if you happen to be thicker than a Snicker! What you put in is what you get out. So much of weight loss is tied to your metabolism, and it's genetically programmed and basically beyond your control. It's why some moms can look at a slice of spelt toast and seemingly gain five pounds, and others can eat eight times a day and still lose weight. Jessica Biel can eat my plate, her plate, and the extra plate of food on the counter and still maintain that slim build without gaining an ounce of fat. Some people are truly blessed in that department. I am not one of them—the junk overflows in my trunk!

When do moms start to really lose the baby weight?

I always say, "Nine up and nine down." It took you nine months to put it on, so to be realistic: it will take at least nine months to get it off and keep it off. If your metabolism and work-out regimen were sloth-like pre-baby, don't expect them to be cheetah-like post-baby. You can't compare your results to women like Jess Biel, who have super-high metabolisms, or women who are compulsive exercisers and can't bear to handle a little junk in their trunk.

The only person you need to compare yourself to is yourself! Set small, achievable goals and celebrate each and every one of them. At this point your focus needs to be only on your hunger; your need to eat good, healthy, clean food; and your baby's nutrition. Don't stress; the weight will come off. Also know that your body totally changes to have that baby. It's like being a virgin. Once the deed is done, there's no going back. You might get your weight down to what it was pre-pregnancy—round of applause!—but your hips will be slightly wider, and you might have scars and stretch marks. (Rubbing shea butter or olive oil on the stretch marks will help.) Think of them as proud reminders of the incredible feat you accomplished to grow that incredible baby inside of your incredible body.

As for your breasts, some go back to the size and shape they were before, and some don't. It's impossible to predict. I've had some moms just totally deflate once they stop breast-feeding and others who lost a lot of elasticity and firmness due to all the suckling and pulling. But that's what breasts are meant to do—nourish your wonderful baby.

Instead of looking at your old wardrobe and crying over not being able to fit into it again, get some transitional clothing—a few outfits that aren't terribly expensive but are comfortable, easy to wash, and make you feel and look good.

Exercising After the Baby Is Born

Our bodies are meant to move. A lot of moms who are fit from regular cardiovascular and strength-training exercise keep up their routines—with their obstetrician's blessing—until the baby is born. If that's you, fantastic. Having strong muscles and a strong heart will help you with the delivery, especially if your core is well developed. If you're sedentary, you should only start a vigorous exercise regime while you're pregnant with your doctor's express permission, especially if you don't want to gain a lot of weight.

Even if you're a professional athlete, you should not exercise until your doctor has given you the go-ahead. Hopefully, you'll be told to start up again at a snail's pace and slowly ease back into it. This is usually around three months after the birth. I think it's better if you wait for six months, unless you were in excellent physical shape before the baby was born. At that stage the baby will be eating solids to supplement your feedings, and you won't have to worry so much about your milk supply.

Regular exercise, however, does not dry up your milk production. As long as you replenish your fluids throughout the day, you will be fine. A lot of women forget to drink more when they exercise, especially around the three-month mark, and this is what has the effect on your milk. Water, water, water is what keeps that milk flowing!

Don't forget that you need to up your calorie count, and working out will burn calories. Eat more when you exercise more.

The Best Exercise Is Gentle Walking

For most moms, walking is the ideal way to get blood pumping. Start slow and go to the corner and back. Add a minute or two every day as you get your strength back. If you like to jog or run and have room for an exercise stroller in your house, use it; they're very stable and meant to be pushed while you're on the move.

GETTING THE SLEEP YOU NEED

Your new constant sleep-wake-sleep-collapse cycle will almost be like Chinese water torture, to fall asleep just as you hear the baby cry. There's just no way to be prepared for a newborn's sleep/feed schedule, and I know you aren't crazy enough to try to figure it out!

Getting enough sleep is going to be way up high on your priority list. If you can't sleep, you can't function. Sleep deprivation is so bad (and so common) that many parents can't even articulate how bone-weary they are. It only takes a few days of constant awakenings, especially if you've just fallen into a deep sleep, for deprivation to set in. If you finally catch the sandman from 3:00 a.m. to 7:00 a.m., that's still not going to be enough, especially if you're breast-feeding and your body needs that extra energy.

Being this exhausted will change your whole demeanor, how you deal with your baby, how you talk to your partner, and how you relate to your friends and family. It can also trigger depression because you're so upset at being tired all the time, and your ability to cope with simple life functions is diminished. Getting woken up from a really deep sleep can trigger a visceral rage that is your brain screaming, *"If you don't get us back in that bed and close our eyes right now . . ."* You won't have your wits about you, and you'll be frustrated as hell.

That's when you start to question everything about your life: When did I become a milking cow? Whose idea was it for me to be a parent? Why am I always the one to do everything around here and no one else is going through this?

Sound familiar?

The Sleepy-time Team

The only way you're going to survive the first month is by having a team you can count on to help you through the night so you can sleep. Adjusting to your new baby-feeding schedule really does take a village.

If you have a baby nurse like me, I will be your Plan A because my role is to be up with the baby, so you can sleep, 24/7. If you don't have someone like me, your team can be your partner, family members, or friends who are night owls. Or you can have people come over during the daytime so you can nap, which is always easier (and less expensive) than getting help at night. Even one person coming over at night every three or four days will make a huge difference, just knowing you can shut the door and hibernate.

Draw up Plan A with your team, but don't have unrealistic expectations—your team also has commitments and needs sleep. Have Plan B ready (other friends to fill in for a night).

Some partners step up to the plate very well, and your Plan A (they help out with the nighttime feedings) will work out perfectly. You'll get a rhythm going that works for you both. Some partners, on the other hand, need to be encouraged. Speak up! This is not the time to tough it out. Just say you need help and work out something that fits both your schedules.

The Perfect Sleep Scenario for Your First Month

My perfect scenario:

+ Do your normal feeds all day long.

+ Train your boobs to go dormant at the 9:00 p.m. or 11:00 p.m. feedings. You'll go to sleep, and your boobs will, too. Going dormant means you don't feed in the middle of the night. Your boobs will slow down on production because they aren't required to show up and show out during those times. But if you're having issues producing milk, going dormant is not an option you'll want to explore because it will only compound the problem.

+ When you get up for that 5:00 a.m. feeding, you'll have ample milk and a really good pump.

+ You should still have more milk at that next feeding than you would normally have.

This system works brilliantly. Babies do just fine having those two bottles you pumped out, and you will get the sleep you need.

As soon as you stop the middle-of-the-night feedings, your breasts will be smart enough to go dormant during that time and produce milk at a slower pace. The only reason they were responding so quickly in the wee hours was because you were doing those feedings.

Your baby will be thrilled to get a nice full tummy from a bottle in the middle of the night and go right back to sleep. This will make you a happier, fully awake person instead of a frustrated zombie.

Sleep When the Baby Sleeps

You can't be the ball boy, the coach, the starting pitcher, the relief, and the umpire . . . all that and a hot dog and a box of popcorn. You need to go to sleep!

If you learn nothing else from this book, sleep when the baby sleeps. That means that you're going to be sleeping in three-hour increments at most. Nap within hearing distance of your baby. Have a comfy bed or sofa near your feeding station or a co-sleeper attached to the side of your bed so you don't have to sleepwalk down the hall when the baby starts to cry.

Do Whatever You Can to Relax

Even when you're not sleeping, you need to chill. Put your sleep needs first. If you're so overtired that you can't wind down, try this:

+ Chamomile tea can help you relax, and it's safe for breast-feeding moms. Any other kind of warm drink will also be soothing.

+ Take a hot bath. You already know how good it is for your baby!

✦ Have someone give you a soothing massage. You deserve it.

✦ Aromatherapy is great, and certain oils like lavender are very relaxing. Get a diffuser to scent the air with sleep-inducing essential oils.

✦ If you have laundry or dishes to do, oh well. They can wait. Your sleep is much more important than an empty sink.

✦ Turn off your electronics, and put your phone on mute. I'm always happy to be that buffer who tells callers that "No, they can't talk right now because they're napping." If you don't have help, change your voicemail and leave a message saying you're sleeping. Send out an SOS to your friends that you're in training and communications might be hit or miss for the next month or so.

✦ Instead of Date Night, have Sleep Night. Figure out how much you would have spent going out to dinner and the movies, and use that money for a sitter or trusted friend who can be there from 9:00 p.m. to 2:00 a.m. Pump before that blessed person arrives to get you through two feedings, so you'll have five hours of blissfully uninterrupted sleep.

Every parent I've worked with eventually figured it out. Their bodies adjusted, and they got into the rhythm of their sleep schedule. As their babies grew, everything got easier. Most of all, they realized they couldn't stick to the same schedule they'd had before the baby was born. Even the non-nappers (and there are a lot of people who find it almost impossible to nap, even when bone-weary) eventually figure it out. So do the night owls, who can't believe they're getting up so early in the morning!

Around the three-month mark, you should start to feel your

energy returning and your sleep improving. You might even wake up one day, feel great, and make plans to go out to dinner with your partner, only to crash later in the day—and be smart enough to cancel. By the fourth month, you probably won't be canceling! Go out and have fun.

chapter twelve

TAKING CARE OF YOUR EMOTIONAL NEEDS

All Celebrity Moms: This section fits all my mommies. From looking for their phones that were in their pocket to leaving groceries in the car because they were so focused on getting in to feed the baby to having to write lists because they felt like their memory got pushed out with the baby—Mommy Brain does not discriminate! They honestly thought they were losing their minds, and I'd just sit back and laugh. Then I'd gently rub their shoulders as they looked at me like, "What the hell!" I'd say, "Sweetheart, this too shall pass. Just relax and you'll get the groove back." When they would find their keys in the freezer, we would laugh and say, "Mommy Brain!"

I was born in 1959 and blessed beyond measure to have had not just a loving family of my own, but also an entire community that had my mother's back. In our neighborhood, once a new mom came home with the baby, our "village" rose to the task of helping take care of her. They bathed and dressed her, cooked for her, and fed her. They took care of her baby when she was napping, and they handed her the baby when she woke up because they knew the importance of taking care of your own child. All these new moms were able to enter into motherhood at a much more glorious, stately, calm-inducing pace rather than just being thrown into the fire.

What has shifted since then? Well, now new mamas are expected to be able to take care of not only the baby, but also themselves. This is a problem.

I want you to read this section and visualize me giving you one of my famous hugs, because Lord knows you need it. Having a baby is physically hard, as you know. Taking care of a baby is even harder. There will be moments of pure bliss and wonder that will thrill you in a way you never thought possible as you gaze down at your gorgeous bundle of love. There will be trials and tribulations that will make you weep and wail from the stress and worry of it all.

Just remember this: *shit happens*. It happens to every new parent. You can't control everything. You can't always prepare for the unexpected, except knowing it will happen sooner or later. Your emotions are going to be all over the place, so remember this too: *you can't do it on your own*. You need to take care of you, and you need help to do it. Ask everyone you can to help take care of you, too. Having a baby nurse, family member, church member, friend, or someone who has had a baby be with you and give you guidance will put you at ease.

THE MANY JOYS OF
MOMMY BRAIN . . . KIDDING!

Before I move along to the tougher emotional stuff, allow me to say a few words about the mush currently floating around in your cranium. Yes, my love, you have Mommy Brain.

I haven't met a mom who didn't suffer from Mommy Brain. Some moms have it in small doses; others have it in overdrive. You'll notice it when you get home from the hospital and are all ready to deal with your C-section or episiotomy. You'll walk into the bathroom, look in the mirror, and say, "Now, what am I supposed to be doing?" You'll feel like you just flushed half your brain down the toilet.

Mommy Brain is what happens when your postpartum hormones are trying to get their act together, coupled with your body trying to get its act together after the birth, made worse by your new schedule, new demands, and lack of sleep. Who wouldn't get all foggy? You can get so forgetful that you'll lose your train of thought midsentence or won't even remember what you were talking about in the first place.

You've got to own your Mommy Brain. It's not going to last forever—it gets better as the months go by. You probably won't see any substantial changes until you make it past the first five months. (If Mommy Brain persists after that point, speak to your doctor so you can get your hormone levels tested.)

It'll give you something to laugh about when your baby is older, like the times you put your eyeglasses in the freezer when you were getting some ice, when you took the cordless phone to the car, or you wore socks and shoes that did not match.

The best way to deal with Mommy Brain is to write yourself notes and To Do lists, avoid juggling too many thoughts at once, complete one task before starting another, and sleep. Put your essential items (purse, keys, wallet, glasses, shoes, etc.) in the same place every single day. That way, your muscle memory will override your Mommy Brain, and you won't wonder why you can't get your act together. Besides, you know how important it is to be organized with all the baby stuff in the house, too. You got this!

MANAGING STRESS

I am so attuned to the needs of new moms by now that I can instantly tell when they are stressed. It's practically radiating off them like sunshine.

New Baby Stress is a given, so I become Mom's confidante, tell Dad how important it is to be his wife's BFF, and keep all the Negative Nellies away from her. When the tears are coming in buckets, the most important thing for me to do is to hug and coddle her, rub her feet, and just let her cry it out while sitting there quietly as a sympathetic ear.

Emily Blunt: "Let me tell you about 'The Nanny Connie Hug.' Here's the deal. As she would say so about herself, it's like you could feel her cover your entire *bloody back* as she simultaneously hugs you and massages your back. I have seen grown men melt in her arms, most of whom she had pulled onto her knee. (She's six feet tall, maybe more, ha-ha!) I myself had collapsed into those arms when feeling overwhelmed, when exhausted, when emotional, when thrilled and celebrating. I have seen friends of mine start to cry when she hugged them, as if she had unlocked something in them that they had held back. She somehow always knew the people who needed to be held the most! And that same sure-handed, loving touch was why my daughters melted into some sort of meditative slumber when she held them. This woman—no joke—could soothe a baby to sleep during a tsunami!"

Stress is one of the biggest problems we all face, especially because so many people don't know how to handle, channel, or cope with it. Often, stress is bubbling along in that new-baby pot until it boils over. New parents explode on each other or their family, or they cry that the baby won't latch and then have a guilt trip because they've lashed out at the people who love them most. There is usually a lot of screaming and frustration. That's when the dreaded "Don't tell me you know how I feel because you don't" scenario plays out. It can be hard to click out of this because you often don't realize just how bad you feel and how badly you're lashing out until the moment has passed.

Managing your job, partner, family, money issues, your own needs, and a tiny infant can push all your wrong buttons. This worries me with moms because chronic stress has a negative effect on milk production. It only takes one stressful day to deplete a week's worth of milk.

Babies are so attuned to you that they will respond to your stress—they can feel it in your body, and it will make them unhappy. Worse, there is a snowball effect that goes from "Okay, I'm trying to cope" to "OMG, help me, I can't take one more day of this, and my baby is gonna starve because my milk isn't flowing." Something has to give!

Own Your Stress

No one can predict how well you will manage the new responsibilities of being a parent, especially a mother. I can give you an overall picture of birth, but I can't tell you that raising your baby is going to be all peaches and cream! The truth is that being a parent is hard as hell. This is especially true if you're the person who pushed that little miracle out. Your body and your emotions are going to take you on a roller coaster ride. Some of the most put-together and competent women I know completely fell apart their first month home, while others sailed through even though they were silently moaning that their stitches were driving them crazy without once telling anyone. I'm sure you had all these grand plans of what you thought your parenting journey was going to look like, but I guarantee you didn't figure in the fact that your baby has a mind of their own. So how can you cope?

+ Own your stress. Don't pretend it's not there. You are not a superhero. You are learning new skills on the job, and the last thing you should do is beat yourself up about it.

   Instead, simply tell yourself, "This too shall pass. Stressing about stress only leads to more stress."

+ Stop trying to wear that S on your chest. You are smart and capable and strong and accomplished. You will figure it out—because you know you don't have a choice.

+ There is no magic pill that will completely alleviate your stress. If you feel like the only way to cope is to self-medicate, it's time to seek some professional help.

+ Denial won't help when you're skipping down the Yellow Brick Stress Road. "I'm good," some parents say with that deer-in-the-headlights look. Bless your heart.

+ If you have a partner on this parenting journey, both of you need to step up to the plate. On a basic level, men tend to deal in black and white, while women deal in black, white, gray, blue, and green with polka dots on top. With some partners, you can be very specific and blunt when you ask for help, but with others you'll have to do some finessing, even when you want to hit them with a "Hell, naw, dawg." Clear, concise communication is a major key to avoiding stress.

+ Sleep. Enough said.

+ Treat yourself. You deserve it.

+ Breathing techniques work. Count slowly while you breathe in and out. (This also prevents you from yelling in the heat of the moment.) There are thousands of breathing, meditation, and self-soothing apps and YouTube videos that will guide you through specific calming techniques.

+ A "village" can be found between you and your partner if they step up the way I hope they will. And a lot of partners do. They can't breast-feed, but they can do everything else. They can run bathwater. They can turn on your favorite TV show or say, "Honey, I'm going to pick up dinner, and then I'm going to get you this and this and that." Just to take the pressure off. Heaven is when someone else makes decisions for you, so you can concentrate on the baby and getting your energy back.

+ No one is a mind reader. You can take a whole lot of the edge off if you just communicate with your partner and they communicate with you. Don't bottle it up; pressure bursts pipes.

    Nagging is not communicating. It only makes things worse. Hit them with the sugar ("Honey, I know you have a lot on your plate right now, but if you could remember to help me with this, it will make me feel a lot better."), not with the salt ("I swear to God, I told you this already. And this is my second time asking."). Always remember you get more with sugar than with salt.

    Two sentences you never want to hear yourself saying are "Why did you do _____?" and "I swear to God, I told you this already. This is my second time asking." You'll get a total shutdown instead of the help you need.

SINGLE PARENTS NEED MORE HELP THAN ANYONE

Raising a child with two parents in the picture is tough; raising a child with one parent can feel damn near impossible. If this is you, give yourself a round of applause! Listen, I lived the single parent story. Although I was blessed to have my village of my family, it was still hard as hell!

As a single parent you don't need to second-guess asking for help because you can't do it on your own, and stress, anxiety, and depression will sneak up on you before you know it. Society does have a way of excluding single parents because they judge them before even knowing their story. However, they need support more than anyone because they don't have a partner to depend on or bounce ideas off of. So be the village. Don't exclude them; embrace them!

Share the Burden

✦ If you're feeling super-sensitive, say so. If a friend says, "How long are you going to be feeding that baby?" they probably mean "How long is it going to take so I can get dinner ready for you and run you a bath?" You will hear "WTH is wrong with you that the baby takes so long to feed?" But that's not what they meant at all. Explain that New Baby Stress makes everything seem much more intense and negative than it really is, and to hear someone put truth to your thoughts of not doing or being enough only makes you retreat and not want to talk to anybody or leave the house.

✦ Tell your friends that sometimes you just need to vent and rant about your nipples pointing south or the consistency of your baby's poop even though you know it makes you sound a little cray-cray. A good friend will nod and smile (and remind you of it ten years later).

+ Be super-specific when your friends offer to help. Often, those who haven't had babies yet don't have a clue what you need, so they do nothing. Ask them to do a food run or set up a diaper delivery online—or just keep you company when you're zoning out in front of the TV.

+ If a friend comes over to give you some precious downtime so you can nap, tell them to let you sleep until the specified time. They can handle the baby should they wake up sooner. Those five extra minutes of you not being shaken out of your boots is so important.

STRESS BUSTING WITH YOUR MOTHER-IN-LAW

One of the most stressful situations I've seen time and again is when the in-laws arrive . . . and don't leave for weeks or even months. If you love them but don't exactly get along— telling yourself you married their child, not them, with all their my-way-or-the-highway child-rearing ideas—you are going to be stressed, with no escape in sight.

Time for a Follow Your Lead conversation. Without one, you'll never forget how Grandma or Grandpa pissed you off when you first came home, and that's not fair. Your baby may end up loving them dearly, and you don't want to still be mad enough to deny them that relationship. As difficult as your in-laws may be, they now have a grandchild who belongs to all of you.

Follow Your Lead, make your house rules clear, and everything will smooth out. Especially when Grandma takes the baby when you need to sleep!

MANAGING ANXIETY

Everyone gets anxious. Hell, I get anxious! It's part of life. Even moms who are smart, competent, and well organized prior to their baby's arrival find themselves acting totally out of character due to anxiety. Society tells moms that they're supposed to magically be back on their feet, with all the baby weight shed overnight, and back to their old life without any worries other than when the diaper shipment's arriving. Hello out there? Who wouldn't be anxious when totally unrealistic expectations are dumped on your Mommy Brain?

Anxiety is an unwelcome guest in your home. Take care of it, and it'll eventually buzz off. Avoid it or deny it, and it'll stay in your house like your least-liked cousin who just doesn't get the hint that the party's over and she has got to get the hell out. Stress that isn't managed can build up and tip over into anxiety—clinically defined as "a nervous disorder characterized by a state of excessive uneasiness and apprehension, typically with compulsive behavior or panic attacks." In other words, your nerves are shot!

Accept the fact that you're going to have irrational moments. Your mantra should be, and repeat after me: "This too shall pass."

Anxiety manifests itself in different ways. The tendency is to assume that anxious people are manic and energetic or have obsessive thoughts and fears. But some moms get very quiet in an attempt to quell their fears, especially if they've had anxiety in the past and are so ashamed about it (which breaks my heart) that they've gotten better at hiding it from their loved ones. When the joviality has gone from a conversation and a mom appears withdrawn and disinterested in being with her family or friends, something is off. Anxiety can also take a physical toll on moms, who might either eat too much or too little or not be able to sleep.

Panic attacks can suddenly appear for seemingly no reason. Your heart rate can drastically increase, you can be sweaty and dizzy, and you can feel very confused—making you think you're having a heart attack. It's very scary because you don't know what's happening to you.

If your anxiety morphs from occasional flashes of panic to constant, chronic worries, you should seek medical advice from your obstetrician or physician. Better to be safe than not do anything, as anxiety can snowball into something major. Ask for a complete blood workup to check your hormone and micronutrient (vitamins and minerals) levels, because if anything is out of whack, it can trigger anxiety symptoms—and then you'd be blaming yourself for something that was completely out of your control. If your doctor suggests therapy, take their advice. Professional guidance and support should give you the tools you need to manage your feelings.

Through it all, make sure you communicate your thoughts and feelings with family members or friends. Don't try to row this boat alone. Even as your baby-care tasks become second nature, you might need more help than you think. And do not hesitate to get professional medical help, because there is no reason for you to suffer.

KEEP ANOTHER JOURNAL TO TRACK HOW YOU'RE FEELING

You're already keeping a feeding log for the baby, so this journal is just for you, your own little confessional. Writing down your feelings is amazingly therapeutic because putting pen to paper allows you to express your thoughts and feelings and get them out of your system. Detailed journals are also helpful for you to reread over time, so you can notice certain patterns or triggers when they're read in sequence.

Buy yourself a beautiful little diary or use the Notepad app on your phone. If you are too tired to write, record that day's feelings on your phone or a digital recorder. Doing so for even a few minutes will make you feel better.

I also suggest you allow your loved ones to read your journal if you are feeling overwhelmed, sad, anxious, or depressed. They know you well and will be able to tell if you're not yourself by the tone and content of your writing. They can also judge if you just got a little anxious one day when the baby was fussy or if you're repeating the same fears over and over. Your partner can also take your journal to the doctor, which can be very helpful if you need medical advice. Often, your loved ones know something isn't quite right, but they don't want to pry and worsen the situation by telling you they think you're anxious or depressed. Handing your best friend or a relative your journal can nip that kind of denial cycle in the bud.

MANAGING DEPRESSION

Postpartum depression shows up in the first three months after the baby is born, when moms have the weight of the family on their shoulders—from worrying about the clothes in the closet not fitting to worrying about Baby's safety when Mommy Brain strikes. As with stress and anxiety, feelings of depression are very common, especially for women who are used to being fully in charge of their lives or who had unrealistic expectations about the demands of infant care. You can go from being competent and organized to frustrated, overwhelmed, and inconsolable in the span of only a few days or weeks.

Being sad, crying all the time, and thinking you'll never get through this doesn't automatically mean you've got postpartum depression. It usually means you're a mom who needs some time to adjust!

In my experience, most of my mothers realized that being depressed was situational and that their feelings would improve when the situation improved. Once they got into the rhythm of child care, got enough sleep, asked for help, and their hormones adjusted back to normal, the depression went away.

During the first few months home, I talk to my moms frequently and keep the line of communication open. I tell funny stories, sit with them when they are alone, and try to get them out of the house to get their hair done or go to lunch with friends.

Clinical postpartum depression, on the other hand, is a serious condition that rarely improves on its own. I've found that it becomes more evident after the first month and the first shock of a new baby and a new schedule is beginning to wear off. The moms I worked with who had it cried all the time, felt like they couldn't get a handle on life, took no pleasure in anything, had trouble eating and sleeping, and, most tellingly, didn't want to be around their babies. When this happens, moms need to seek prompt medical attention from their doctors and/or a therapist, especially if they have chronic feelings of helplessness and worthlessness, or if their moods darken and deepen. Get a complete physical and blood workup to test for any hormonal issues and micronutrient deficiencies; imbalances or low levels can lead to depression. Antidepressants might be recommended, some of which can't be taken if you're breast-feeding. In this case, it is much better to bottle-feed your baby and get better than to deny what's happening to you.

chapter thirteen

YOUR RELATIONSHIP WITH YOUR PARTNER

Jessica Biel: "When Nanny Connie came into our lives, she worked with me day by day to understand that what my child and my family needed more than organic diapers and gallons of breast milk was balance. She supported the somewhat extreme lifestyle that we had chosen for our family while teaching us about how real life exists in the middle, somewhere in the gray area of the world.

"She comforted my husband and me when we were tortured by sleepless nights and were zombies of our former selves. She would force us out of the house for date nights because it was important to connect again as adults, or 'pay the mortgage' as she called it. Thank you, Jesus!" As nanny likes to say.

Your beloved partner just watched you grow through nine months of pregnancy, painfully pop out a baby, and develop nice perky breasts overnight, and now your hormones are flying all over the place. Right now, you need them more than ever.

Teamwork Makes the Dream Work

Everyone has to step up their game and be willing to chip in in areas where they normally don't. Just because there's a new baby in the house doesn't mean the world stops. Food still has to be made, gas still has to be put in the car, bills still have to be paid (I'm sure you got the picture). Ultimate teamwork is making sure everyone gets some uninterrupted sleep! Trust me, sleep deprivation will lead to heads rolling all over the place. This is especially important if you were the one who pushed that little person out. You are dealing with aches and pains, body issues, and stress, and the last thing you need is someone not pulling their weight. You need your partner to be there for you emotionally and physically.

To strengthen your bond as a couple, you need to specify who does what, talk to each other, and make time for each other.

Practice Makes Perfect

I can't stress this enough: If you want your partner to be involved, then you have to let them do things their way. You can't ask for help and then criticize them when they do something differently than you do. Just bite that tongue.

If they put a diaper on backward, no biggie. They changed the diaper, and that's what counts. And if the diaper they put on backward leaks all over them, they'll do better next time. You have to let them mess up so they can learn.

You know your partner is dog tired from fighting the outside world all day. Trust me, they know you've had the baby all day, but shoving your child into your partner's arms immediately after they walk in the door and saying "I've had the baby all day" is grounds for an argument. Hell, I'd fuss at you, too! Give them a minute. Let them change and wash their hands. They've got to get those hands clean before they touch the baby, anyway!

Remember, this phase is temporary. Teamwork means compromise, a constant give and take. Some days will be incredibly joyful and satisfying, and some days will be so bad that exhaustion will cover you like an umbrella. When you love each other—and don't be afraid to affirm your love and affection, even when (actually, especially when) your partner is being a pain in your ass—you're in it together. The baby will get bigger and need fewer feedings, you will sleep more, and you will feel like a family. Because you are a family.

All Aboard

Buckle up! The train has left the station, and there's no turning back now—or, as some of you like to say, "This shit just got real!"

Don't stress too much, because this sista has your back, and if you listen to what I am telling you, you will be back to your vices before you know it! And when six weeks come around, she will be ready to, and I quote, "Turn off the lights and light a candle."

The new addition is finally here, and you are probably still as high as if you had had the epidural yourself. Now, here's where you have to play your cards right. You must understand that nothing you do for the next two weeks will be right, so don't overthink it. When she starts talking, don't look at your phone or bury your head in the television, and try not to agree to what she's saying without processing what's coming out of her mouth. When the time comes for you to take the baby to their first checkup, and she says she told you about the appointment and you agreed, that's the second trip to the doghouse. Oh, I didn't tell you about the first? Well, let me back it up! You've packed her and the baby up, gotten everyone home from the hospital, and now you are expecting her to be back to normal. Trust me, that's the first trip to that proverbial doghouse.

I have seen it all, and at this point, nothing surprises me. I've had dads who thought they were on vacation because I was there, and the day I left was when he decided to start learning the process. It's too late by then!

Take the time to learn how to put the diaper on and care for your baby. When your partner is changing the baby, don't turn and walk out of the room. You'll just build another room in your doghouse when you say, "That's not my job." Open mouth and insert foot.

I had a father once tell me he was never going to change his daughter. So, one day we were watching college football together, and it was coming up on halftime. I made the remark that one day his daughter would be on the sidelines as a cheerleader or in the band. He turned to me and said, "The only way my daughter would be at the games is with the season tickets I'll be buying her to sit next to me." I laughed as he gave me his whole explanation behind it and why he would not change that diaper. He was a frat boy in college, and with his daughter, protective mode kicked in. He wanted her pocketbook to remain her pocketbook and couldn't wrap his head around any man including himself being anywhere near it. I stopped laughing long enough to tell him he didn't need to say any more and added that parenthood had a way of putting you in your place. He nodded, but I could tell he was tuning me out.

I was down to my last seven days, and I told him I was leaving soon, and it was time for him to learn how to change his daughter's diaper. He finally responded, "Oh, all right, Nanny Connie." I taught him, and on the last day, he did the bath-time routine, too. While putting her diaper on, he started to cry. I asked him what was wrong, and he said, "Karma has a way of getting you back." I said, "YEP, and in this case, I am karma's best friend."

I say this because no matter what your past life was, you are now a parent, and you can't take it lightly. Know your stuff so when Mom is gone and something happens, you at least have some idea of what's going on.

Keep your head in the game. This is the World Series, the Masters, the Final Four, the NBA Finals, the Stanley Cup Finals, and the Super Bowl. (I hope you're getting the picture!)

Take one day a week to learn all the gadgets, put them together, read the manuals, and set up the equipment so when you are called upon, your partner doesn't worry or wonder if you know what the hell you're doing. That's being a team player, and that's what they're looking for. Don't just go to the baby store because they asked—go because you want to be a willing participant. If you picked out the car seat, take it upon yourself to go by the fire station or police station and learn how to secure it. When your partner sees you taking the initiative to do things, they will relax and stop adding to that Honey, Do This Now list.

Don't fake it until you make it. Don't tell your partner one thing when you really don't know what the hell you're talking about. Along will come that argument about lack of trust that you brought on yourself.

Sit down with your partner in the very beginning, make a plan, and stick to it. Go a little overboard with helping. If it's your first time, share the load, and if it's your second time, share the load.

As young adults at family gatherings, my cousins and I would sit and listen to Mu talk about how important family was. She would say, "If you don't want children, then you should leave them in Nuttsville, because it is a responsibility." Being in our twenties, we all would laugh and consider it a joke—until years later when we realized that becoming a parent is a life-altering situation that should never be taken lightly.

It Takes Two

So much attention is given to new moms that their partners often get overlooked. Although they won't be going through the physical healing you will, they are still dealing with sleep deprivation, stress, anxiety, and maybe even depression. You shouldn't assume they are all peachy-fine if they don't say anything. They might love you and the baby so much that they don't want to add to your stress.

Minimizing your partner's needs is a guaranteed recipe for disaster. Don't neglect your partner. That relationship was important enough to nurture before the baby came along, and it is even more important now. As tired as you are, you need to make the extra effort to arrange a nice, quiet, and loving time to sit down and have a heart-to-heart. Remember, you get more with sugar than with salt.

Sometimes Dads Need a Little Bit More Guidance Than You Might Think. . . .

One of my first live-in jobs was for a family who lived in a cul-de-sac in a friendly neighborhood where everyone seemed to be having babies at the same time. I moved from one family to the next, usually for three weeks or the first month, getting to know the couples before I started working for them.

One night, a mom I had already worked for decided it was time for Dad to watch the baby, who was three weeks old, for the first time. She told all her friends he was in charge, just in case (and so they could keep an eye on him), and set off for her Junior League meeting.

Dad was totally cool with it. He listened to her instructions and then promptly forgot what she said. The baby went down, and about half an hour later, Dad realized he was out of cigarettes. Off he went to the gas station, about a five-minutes' drive away. One of the neighboring moms saw him there and was a bit surprised. She asked Dad if the meeting was over, and he said no, but that he and the baby were doing good. She peered into the car and didn't see the baby and started to panic.

"Oh, don't worry," he said. "The baby's fine. I can hear him right here on the monitor."

Dad, in his infinite wisdom, thought the baby monitor would work if he took it out of the house. All he heard was static, of course. He thought it was fine. Mom did not when she got home.

The baby slept through the drama, but that was the end of Dad's baby duty for quite some time. Bless his heart.

GETTING BACK INTO THE GROOVE

If you want to add an addition to your doghouse, all you have to do is ask your partner this question: "When can we get back to paying the mortgage?" as I like to call it. Trust me, she'll help you build that addition quicker than you can finish that sentence! Now, you may ask me what is "paying the mortgage." Well, it is definitely not paying the rent—that is something you do before you get married. You see, when you are married, everything is long lasting and intimate. So "paying the mortgage" is that "turn out the lights; let's get closer" time.

Mommy Needs Time to Heal

The issue with resuming a healthy sex life isn't so much the physical healing but the emotional healing.

If you continued to have regular sex throughout your pregnancy, it's a bit easier to ask your partner to wait. Often, that last little round of sex makes a couple feel more intimately connected. A lot of moms-to-be, though, feel physically uncomfortable as well as fearful of undressing in front of their other halves. They're not used to the bigger boobs or their swollen bellies as they morphed into a vessel to give birth to a human being. I always tell them they have to be okay with what the good Lord gave them—and that's their body!

Partners need to understand and respect each other, be mindful, and be patient. Many new moms are upset with their bodies, and that isn't exactly a turn-on. It takes a woman nine months to grow the baby, and it's going to take her at least a good three to four months to come around to feeling like the woman she was before.

From all the frank discussions I've had with parents, nearly all the women have told me that their partners' understanding and support sped up the healing process. What they wanted wasn't so much the invigorating sex they'd had pre-baby, but to start out slowly with caressing, cuddling, and emotional and physical support. The last thing you need to do is point out that extra roll she may have gained. If anything, you need to admire that roll like it's your favorite body part! Trust me, she's already her biggest critic at this point and the last thing she needs is for you to validate her critiques.

When they're ready, hopefully new moms will realize sex after Baby can be really fun. It doesn't have to be as intense as it was—this is not the Kentucky Derby! Don't come out the gate like you did when you were twenty-one and a young thoroughbred. You're a parent now, your body has changed, and you're not going to know how your body is going to respond to sex.

Go slower at first. Use this time to get creative. You might still be sore or have a backache, so certain positions you liked before the baby aren't going to feel as comfortable. Take the lead, say what feels good and what doesn't, and relax.

Most of all, be respectful of each other. That's what marriage or partnership is all about. It's how some couples stay together for fifty or sixty years—they realize that how they had sex when they were twenty-five is not how they had it at thirty-five or forty-five. They are always mindful of their partner's needs and desires and have no qualms about communicating these needs and desires. They want to make each other feel amazing, loved, and adored. Being a parent is forever—and you want to be with your mate forever, too. Trust each other, set the mood, and go for it.

Inevitably, of course, just when Marvin Gaye is crooning and you're finally getting it on, the baby is going to start crying. Get used to it, because it's gonna happen whether you're in bed or not. Simply get dressed, feed the baby, and expect to find your partner snoring when you crawl back into bed!

To avoid this as best you can, try to time your intimate encounters around the baby's feeding. Starting ten minutes before the baby is due to wake up is going to leave you all frustrated. I know it's hard to realize that the little prince or princess is now in charge of the kingdom, but this phase won't last. Soon the heir apparent will be sleeping through the night, and you can get back into the groove. Just remember to lock the door!

If your libido is low, don't stress yet. Your hormones have to reset, and you've got a lot on your mind. Listen, sex is not going to be high on your list of things to do (even if your partner doesn't quite feel the same!). If you're still feeling sexually blah after three or four months, talk to your physician and get that blood work done to check your hormone levels. If your period is back to normal, your estrogen and progesterone levels should be okay, but your thyroid and adrenals might not, which often accounts for loss of libido.

Like a Kid in a Candy Store

When your breasts are engorged with milk, you might see a glowing light in your partner's eyes, a very special little twinkle because of your nice rack. They are going to be like a kid in a candy store, so be prepared! The best part of it is having all hands on deck will definitely stimulate your milk production. You see, your ducts won't know if the signals they're getting are from a baby or your partner. (You've likely noticed this in a store when you heard a baby cry from five aisles over and had an instantaneous letdown.)

Be aware that a breast-feeding mom's breasts are going to be very tender. They're getting worked like they've never been worked before, and the nipples, especially in the early stages of breast-feeding, are going to get cracked and sore. It's all about following your lead and listening to you.

chapter fourteen

YOUR RELATIONSHIPS WITH YOUR FAMILY AND FRIENDS

Brooke Shields: *When Grier was born, Brooke made sure she balanced her time between both girls. Although she was sensitive to making sure Rowan had her quality time, she didn't allow that child to fully wrap her around her finger.*

I would often sit out on the porch with baby Grier because of the old bilirubin count, and even after we got a handle on her count, we loved sitting out there, enjoying quiet moments together. One evening the entire family sat out on the porch. I was holding the baby, and Rowan was getting the undivided attention of both parents. Eventually big sis's curiosity started to get the best of her. You see, Rowan had already checked the situation out earlier and then made her move: so she bypassed me and went straight to her mom.

She mustered all the cuteness she could find and qui-etly asked her mom if she could hold the baby. Brooke and I saw where this was headed, and Brooke just smiled at me. I invited Rowan over so she could ask me the same question. Now, Grier was very peacefully sleeping across my lap. So, when Rowan came over with her cute little self and asked very shyly if she could hold her sister, I gave her my answer—the rules she loved so much. The more I talked, the more that little head turned. She didn't want to hear about the baby being asleep or that she had to wash her hands. All she heard was the "blah, blah, blah, blah . . ." of Char-lie Brown adults. Rowan went back to her mom's lap, and Brooke asked her, "What did Nanny Connie say?" and without missing a beat, Rowan looked Brooke square in the eye and said, "She said NO!"

All that cute pent-up fury gave us all a good laugh.

You can't choose your family, but you can choose your friends. Dealing with them is an integral part of your life. This is your time to let the people who love you help you. There are always going to be pitfalls and ups and downs with a tiny baby in the house, so being prepared for them is half the battle. You're only as strong as your weakest link, so make that link strong and durable.

ASK FOR HELP!

+ You need to admit you are a fallible human being. You are only one person and have only two hands, yet you are now thinking for two people. One of those is a little person who can't do anything more than cry . . . and the last time you checked, you're speaking English, and the baby is speaking in tongues.

+ Stop putting that *S* on your chest—you'll have another thirty-some years to do that!

+ Go to friends and family who are reliable. Anyone who pulls the "So sorry I can't come" at the last minute is off the list.

+ Ask those at your church or house of worship for help. Most of the worshippers are going to be super-excited to help you, and they'll want to give from the heart. I'll bet a lot of them would never dream of taking any payment, simply because they are good souls who love babies and feel blessed you asked them for assistance.

+ If your budget is tight, look for high school or college students in need of extra cash. Don't hire them as sitters, but as helpers or assistants who can do various tasks for you. Someone who can come over for an hour to help with the laundry each week and makes you laugh when they tell you about their teenage antics is worth their weight in gold.

+ Don't micromanage your friends who come to help. If the clothes aren't folded the way you like or the towels are not stacked in the linen closet the way you stack them, deal with them later. You need a nap!

+ Show this to your friends or find a nice, gentle way to share it: whoever comes over to help is there to do the task you asked them to do, not to start running their mouths. You are not capable of dealing with their problems because having to listen to them is as bad as not having any help. Your friends should stay within their boundaries and simply be friends. Nothing more and nothing less. After the task is done, they should ask politely if they can do anything else, and if you're okay, they should turn their lil' butts around and walk out that door. You can catch up on everything else they want to talk about when the baby is older and you're getting all the sleep you need.

✦ When in doubt, take a chill pill and let it go. Learn to pick your battles. The battle you're fighting is with energy depletion and sleep deprivation, so save your strength for them.

Handing Your Baby Over to a Grandparent

Handing your baby over to a grandparent can be tricky to navigate. You need to be clear about feeding times and teach them your nighttime routine, which will minimize any sleeping or feeding disruptions. It can be an especially interesting balancing act if you have multiple grandparents and children. To make this transition a little easier:

✦ Make a visit calendar and stick to it. This way, there are no schedule conflicts, and everyone can plan accordingly.

✦ Make sure each grandparent has that special individual time with each grandchild. Those relationships are so important.

✦ Think ahead. Have your parents or in-laws choose a special hobby that piques both their and your children's interests. Building their own unique relationship with their grandchild is key.

WHEN THERE ARE ALREADY SIBLINGS

Dealing with siblings can be scary, sweet, methodical, manipulative, heartwarming, or all of the above at the same time! Adding a new baby to the mix can trigger feelings of abandonment, throw off your schedule, and be completely exhausting. But the emotion that tends to rear its little green eyes most often is jealousy.

Jealousy can come about as soon as you announce there is going to be a little sister or brother who will never go away, or during the birth when the siblings realize you weren't kidding. It's cool for the first few days because they are getting royal treatment as if it were their birthday or some big holiday. Then reality hits!

At that point, it's time to sit down with the older ones and teach them about sharing and caring. Oh, the siblings will listen to you very carefully . . . but the eyes and the pull-away mean they're thinking, *Oh, I heard you, but that's not happening. Yes, I know you are the parent, but when you're not looking,"* their Kevin Hart voice kicks in, *"'You gone learn today!'"* Yep, some older siblings can be methodical with their intentions.

Here's where you're going to implement chess, not checkers. You have to be three moves ahead, because that sibling has gotten older and has had time to plot ways they can torture the younger ones. Create rules, stick to them, and don't accept anything less from your kids. They will come to understand and then appreciate and love their sibling, but you are going to have to put your wading boots on. There will be many, and I mean many, days where you will question your sanity. But remember you are the parent! You did nothing wrong; you just have to continue to do what you've been doing. Siblings are smart little cookies. You just have to be that much smarter.

HEY, LADY!

I once worked for a family in a very small house where the baby's room was literally the parents' bathroom. They had a little boy named Tyler, who was coming up on two, and his baby sister had just come home. I would play with Tyler to give Mom time with the baby and to help her figure out, as all moms with older children have to, how to deal with two kids. Tyler was starting to use his words, but he was a thumb-sucker. So, it was kind of hard to hear him clearly—except when he said, "Hey, Lady," which is what he called me.

Cut to when it was time for me to leave, and Mommy was upset because her support was about to go, and the anxiety had set in. Mommy told Tyler to come out and say good-bye to me. I was going over the baby's schedule with Mommy and telling her to make sure she ate her lunch and that everything was going to be fine. As we talked, I heard this voice in the background going, "Hey Lady!" That "Hey Lady!" started to escalate. "Tyler, Nanny Connie's about to leave," his mom told him. "Come and say good-bye to her."

Tyler looked at me, peered back in the bed, looked at me and peered back in the bed again. Then with a very clear voice he said, "Hey, Lady! You forgot something!" He pointed at his sister and said again, "You forgot something!" Meaning his sister! His poor mama just melted and started crying.

"Don't worry," I reassured her. "It's going to be okay."

"No, it's not!" she wailed. "Not only are you leaving me, but my son hates my daughter!"

"It's okay, sweetheart. They are going to be fine," I told her, then gave her a kiss, hugged her neck, and off I went.

I checked in on her that same day and I could hear her relief as she told me Tyler was doing just fine with his sister.

Just Be the Parent to All the Siblings

On some days you will feel like a drill sergeant, and I know that's not what you're trying to be. But being a parent requires you to wear many hats, and if you wear this hat when it's needed, you don't have to wear it for long. You can't always be their friend, but you always have to be their parent.

I'm not saying that all siblings are going to tap dance on your nerves. There are some siblings who are as good as gold from day one, and thirty years later they are still good as gold. They never had any issues, and that's great. These siblings are a part of that 1 percent club. For the other 99 percent, this is where you come in with a few simple strategies to make everything easier:

✦ Talk about your pregnancy with your children the day you really start to show. It won't make much sense unless they can see something that will stick in their sweet little heads.

✦ Give the kids plenty of visuals. There are lots of wonderful picture books you can read aloud at night that will help the kids relate to your growing belly.

✦ When the baby is kicking, let the siblings put their hands on your belly. They love doing that, and it makes the baby seem more real.

✦ Start talking to the kids about how they were as infants. Show them how you looked when you were pregnant with them. Let them look at all their baby photos and your journals.

✦ Have a plan in place weeks before your delivery date for someone trusted and loved to watch your kids while you're in the hospital.

✦ Giving your kids special gifts or treats "from the baby" can make them feel a lot better about the new arrival.

Don't assume girls are going to be more loving or interested in the baby than boys will. The bond between siblings can be fierce, no matter what the gender, and some of the most loving relationships I've seen are between a big brother and his little siblings.

No matter how much you talk to little kids and how often they see you breast-feeding, it can take a while for it to sink in, like it did with Tyler.

A new baby can trigger resentment and feelings of abandonment and anxiety in little kids who still need you and can't understand why you aren't as available as you used to be. I can't say this enough: Don't try to transition anything; any change to their routine is guaranteed to cause problems. Don't take away the bottle. Don't start potty training. Don't put them in the "big kid" bed because you need the crib. Don't take them out of their room. Keep things as they were, which makes kids feel secure when you, their number-one security blanket, aren't giving them the same cuddles and nighttime reads you used to. Let them have their stuff— they're going to need it more than ever, and there's nothing wrong with it.

Expect your kids to unravel. It's always hard for small children to share, and sharing you is the hardest of all. Let your children cry if they need to, and they will learn to deal with their emotions.

Include the kids as much as you can in as many baby-centered activities as you can. Read to them when you're reading to the baby. Ask for help with bath time. Let them give the baby a bottle if they're strong enough.

Set aside one-on-one time with your kids, and don't send them off to the grandparents or playdates to get them out of your hair. This is a must. The baby will be happy to have anyone do the feedings and baths and burping while you're playing with the kids the way you used to. Like Tyler, the siblings will need as much attention as you can spare.

Stick to your schedule. Little children like predictability. This will keep you from spreading yourself too thin and becoming so overwhelmed that both you and your milk suffer.

Tell yourself "This is just a phase," because, guess what? It is. Little children love babies, even attention-hogging babies. As soon as the baby is old enough to respond to the big brother or sister, you should see an immediate change in their relationship—one that will warm your heart and ease your fears that they won't get along. You have plenty of years for that to happen!

LET THE SIBLINGS BE BIG BROTHERS AND SISTERS: THEY CAN DO IT!

Remember Ashley and her size-H breasts? Three years after she pumped and pumped and pumped, she had another son, Bryant. I nicknamed him Baby Sugar because he was sweet as pie.

"I had a hard time separating myself from my precious three-year-old Thomas, but Connie would set me straight like only she could. She would say, 'Now, he can go on up and get his own PJs and toothbrush; you stay down here and feed this baby.' I would have cried or screamed at my own mom for reprimanding me like that, but with Connie, I could only laugh. She is the only person I know who has that quality of setting you straight without any hurt feelings."

Thomas was thrilled when he realized how much he could accomplish on his own. He was perfectly capable of doing tasks his mother did for him because she loved babying him—but with a newborn in her arms, one baby was enough!

DEALING WITH ADVICE

Now that your baby's here, you'll be getting even more advice. But advice is just advice; it's not a mandate. How do you differentiate between helpful advice and bogus advice?

+ Listen to the advice giver and ask for specific details if you have questions. Even advice dispensers who go on and on and on might still have one good nugget in a twenty-minute monologue about butt wipes. You never know. If it sounds worth a try, go for it. If it sounds ludicrous, smile and then forget it.

+ Pick out the best bits (such as where to buy diapers online or which mobiles are the most interesting) and disregard the rest. Don't try to take someone's full plan of a mega-mansion and try to apply it to an apartment—it's not going to fit.

+ Assume that whatever worked for friends might not work for you. Even if they say it's my way or the highway, there are plenty of other highways. Anyone who says, "You must do it this way" rarely has advice you'll need. The only thing you must do is what's best for you and your baby.

+ Do your own homework, and if it doesn't work, readjust.

+ The all-purpose, always-handy replies:

  + "Thank you. That's really good advice." Even if you know it isn't.

  + "I have heard that, and that's so sweet of you to share it with me."

  + "I will keep that in mind."

You get more with sugar than with salt. No one has to know that you'll delete everything they just said from your brain five minutes later!

This even happens to me—all the time. I give my advice to my moms, and they say, "Oh, I'll keep that in mind." I know right then and there that it goes straight over their heads. It's up to you to decide what to do. At times, I know I've been blown off, but sometimes after they have a chance to process my comments, they reconsider, come back to me, and ask more questions. I love when that happens.

DEALING WITH SOCIAL MEDIA

I was a little girl when Neil Armstrong set foot on the moon. A whole big group of us were hovering around the TV, and we heard the now-famous words, "One small step for man, one giant leap for mankind." I clearly remember sitting there in awe, thinking that a real live man was standing on the moon at that very moment, and then Walter Cronkite said, "Life as we know it will never be the same." How right he was! Because that opened up the Pandora's box that has brought us to the digital revolution. To me, social media was conceived on that day, and we can't put the technology that now shapes our world back in the box. But we can know how to control and understand it better.

Social media can be an amazing way to get and share information, to connect with friends, or to find that perfect onesie. But it can also be a black hole of time wasting with so-called experts in online forums.

If you can't get through a meal without sneaking peeks at your phone every time it vibrates, this will set a terrible example for your child and sell them short when they realize you pay more attention to a phone than you do to them.

Nothing makes me want to go stand in traffic more than when I see parents and nannies pushing strollers or their babies in swings, heads down, lost in their phones. Their babies are looking at them, yet they are looking at something else. You can't push a stroller while trying to post to your Snapchat story. Or taking a selfie when the light's just turned green.

Instead, choose your child. Every day, you should ask yourself, Did I choose my child today? I am very lucky I was able to raise my daughter before the social media age; now we are thought of as dinosaurs if we're not digitally connected. I could choose her without worrying about a cell phone dinging 24/7.

Social Media After Baby

Once your baby arrives, you're going to have to shift gears. Believe me when I tell you that you won't have the energy to scroll through your newsfeeds. Start getting yourself in the habit of logging off now because this is what it's going to be like once your baby arrives.

Yes, it can be truly amazing to be globally connected, to find old friends, and to hit the Dr. Google button and get instant answers to questions you have about diaper rash or acid reflux. But the downside to social media is the stupidity people feel free to spout online, often saying things they'd never dream of saying to a person's face. So, while there are countless forums and advice groups for parents that can be incredibly helpful when you're up at 3:00 a.m. and want to learn more about sleeping through the night from parents who've been there, all it takes after fifty great answers to your questions is one Negative Nelly who goes off on you and makes your blood pressure shoot through the roof.

✦ Warn your friends that you are taking a social media hiatus while you adjust to the baby. Tell them to text you if they need you, but to please be understanding if you don't get back to them right away. It's not about them—your baby needs you more right now.

+ There are bullies everywhere who will argue that the sky is green and your baby is doomed by having you as a parent. Ignore and block them. Don't take it personally.

+ Take some time to find support groups about specific issues, which tend to filter out some of the crazies. Ask like-minded friends you trust for recommendations that line up with your values as a parent. If, for example, you're looking for naturopathic advice, don't go on a mainstream medical page where you'll get lost in the clutter and think everything you're doing is absolutely wrong. There is no shortage of advice—good, bad, dogmatic, and nutty—and it's up to you to take what you need and ignore the rest.

+ It's almost impossible to have nuance online—certainly not in the way you'd have it with a face-to-face conversation. Think before you type.

+ Be aware of the Instagram and Facebook Syndrome, where everybody else looks so perfect and seemingly has their lives together. Believe me, they're not posting the baby screaming in the corner five minutes before they snapped the photo. Avoid scrolling when you're feeling vulnerable, roll your eyes at the Photoshopping, and move on.

Privacy Concerns

Think very carefully about what you want to share online, because it will be up there forever.

+ Consider changing privacy settings on your profiles.

✦ Tell everyone who's taken or will take photos of your baby how much you do or do not want those photos shared.

✦ Keep in mind geotagging, and never share photos that display your address or any other personal information. No strangers need to know where you and Baby live.

✦ Your baby is going to be the most beautiful and delicious thing you have ever seen, but you can never know who's looking at your social media. Even the most innocent photo of your baby's naked tushie can be turned into child pornography.

✦ Don't overshare. Password-protect your blog if you have one. You can create private Instagram accounts as well as Closed or Secret groups on Facebook where you can freely share photos and other information with only those you know and trust.

YOUR FRIENDSHIPS WILL CHANGE

Going from *The Hangover* to *The Partridge Family* will be a huge shift for your friends, especially those without children. They can feel that while you're gaining a new little person in your life, you're losing them at the same time. New parents can be surprised at how little time they have for their friends, and friends can be perplexed that their previously reliable BFF has disappeared. This can be very, very painful, particularly as women's close friends are often each other's lifelines of sanity and unconditional love.

Parents tend to get a new circle of friends and want to spend time with them for company and advice, especially when on the same feeding schedule. Experienced friends can be a serious blessing in the rough, early stages, reassuring you that you're not a complete failure as a parent when you put on a diaper backward or can't figure out how the monitor works. As the baby hits new milestones, they will be the first to understand how important that is and will be thrilled to spend hours discussing various colors of poop, brands of diapers, and where the onesies are on sale. Your friends without children can't share in that same sort of excitement and commiseration.

The best way to deal with this is to have a transition time. Make it clear to your friends that this is a temporary phase, and you won't be able to pick up the phone or answer texts as quickly as you used to.

+ Admit that you need to be selfish and learn the best way to take care of your baby and that you'll be wrapped up in your own world for a few weeks—but that doesn't mean you don't care about or want to see them. True friends will understand and come through for you. They know Baby will always come first.

+ Tell your friends how important they are to you and how you don't want anything to interfere with your friendships or make them feel like less-than-perfect friends.

+ As you would with your other children, try to make plans with your friends if you're up to it, and try really, really hard to do so at a time when you won't have to cancel. Call in a favor from a family member who's been dying to watch the baby or use a trusted babysitter. Make plans for an early dinner or invite your friend over for dinner, which might be a better option at first, because sitters can cancel, the baby could be fussy, or you might have a hard time leaving the baby at home.

Going on a hiatus for a little bit can actually make your friendship stronger in the long run, because you won't anger or hurt those you can't deal with now. It's very hard to be fair to everybody, and your child-free friends can't share the unique language you have as a parent.

You might also be surprised by the dynamic of having two separate sets of friends—your old ones and your new, parent ones. You're the common denominator who can put these two groups together, but you have to be prepared that they might not get along—and be okay with that. Only you can figure out a balance where these friends don't pull you in two different directions. You can't do parent stuff all the time. You need your old friends to remind you who you were, and you need your new friends to help you grow into who you'll become as a parent.

Unfortunately, some of your friends can become surprisingly jealous you have a baby for any number of reasons. If you notice a change, don't be afraid to speak on it. A lack of communication will kill any relationship, and if it's a friendship worth having, the two of you will figure out what's best for you. And if that means taking some time apart, so be it. It's better to have a short mutual separation than a nasty lifetime split. But also be prepared for a long-term split. Remember everything has a season, and it's okay if that relationship has served its purpose. This is human nature, and you have to chew the meat and spit out the fat.

Having a baby makes you much less selfish as a person, but you have to become more selfish with your time. Set boundaries, because you can't please everyone. But you can please yourself and your partner by making sure you have the time and energy to care for your baby.

conclusion

YOU'RE ON YOUR WAY!

Well, the bottles are loaded, the diapers are refilled, both you and the baby have eaten, and it is time for your next nap. Your next scheduled medication is in an hour, and your dinner from your in-laws will be over around six. On Tuesday, the baby has their second round of shots. Remember to preload that diaper bag and leave at least thirty minutes early—you'll be on your own this time.

It is time for me to hit the road.

Now, I will call to check in and let you know when I make it home, but for now, get some rest; all is well.

These are the lines I frequently tell my parents as the front door quietly closes behind me and my time has come to an end. Although I know all of my parents can fly solo when I leave them, it is still a bittersweet moment. It feels like I'm losing a best friend. As Mu would tell me, "If you don't get those tears when you're leaving, then you didn't do your job." I feel just the same right now! Writing a conclusion is very hard for me simply because I feel like we are just getting started. I've heard from so many parents who struggle with the same issues, and it's as if we've all been walking around aimlessly, waiting for someone to show us the right direction or lead the pack. Now that you've read this book, I hope you understand that I'm not the leader—we all are.

That's what parenthood is all about. We are leaders! We are all a part of the village.

Growing up, it wasn't just my parents who raised me, but also my grandparents and everyone I came into contact with. From my front door to my church door, everyone had a hand in raising and teaching me. They were my village. They taught me about foundations. I pray that this book will help parents understand the importance of building a foundation and securing those first layers so our children can carry it with them forever.

I have been blessed over three decades to travel around Europe with my families, and seeing the great works and frescoes of Da Vinci and Michelangelo left me in awe. Their art reflected the love, nurturing, and dedication these artists poured into them. They reminded me so much of what it takes to be a parent. Your children are a reflection of your love, nurturing, and dedication. Now it is time to see one of the greatest works to have been bestowed upon us thrive: being parents to your baby and watching your little one grow.

Thank you for becoming a part of the village as we set the cornerstone of its foundation. May we all continue to hold one another's hands and hold one another up as parents. I can't wait to see you thrive in this adventure! God bless!

Join the Village!

Aim your camera at Nanny Connie's logo and let your favorite Hollywood stars tell you why Nanny Connie is Hollywood's most loved nanny.

Join the village by uploading your own testimony on the app. Who knows, you may see yours featured along with Nanny Connie's Hollywood testimonies.

acknowledgments

First, I give honor to God and the shoulders I stand on. This book is not only a culmination of my more than thirty-year career but the beginning of another chapter in my journey.

To my village, all of you know who you are. Thank you for the nudge to come from behind the scenes. Thank you for pointing me in the right direction when I couldn't tell my left from my right. Thank you for handing me tissues whether it be from tears of frustration or joy. Thank you for every encouraging call, text message, video chat, email, and letter. This journey has been filled with twists and turns, and you've been there to guide me through every one. Although I'm just starting, everything I've been through thus far has only reaffirmed my belief that it truly takes a village. I don't have the words to express the sincerity of my thanks to my village.

To my talented book agent, Alan Nevins, your personality, insight, energy, and work ethic are second to none. You have gone above and beyond your title in helping me through this process. I sincerely thank you for seeing me and believing in me. To my Simon and Schuster and Gallery Books family, thanks for helping a dream that started more than eight years ago a reality. Thank you, Jennifer Bergstrom, for taking a chance on me. I am eternally grateful for your belief in me. My rock star editor, Lauren McKenna, your confidence, patience, encouragement, support, and reassurance have been invaluable. The dream team: Jennifer Robinson and Diana Velasquez, thank you for making sure I was on the right platforms to share my message and book. Teamwork makes the dream work—thanks Sara Quaranta for the time you spent making sure all the t's were crossed and i's were dotted.

My great-grandmother Lucy always told me to do what I love. Thank God I heeded her wisdom . . . Blessed!